Success Strategies for Helping Girls With Dyslexia and Reading Difficulties

Why Can't My Daughter Read?

Ellen Burns Hurst, Ph.D.

PRUFROCK PRESS INC.
WACO, TEXAS

Acknowledgments

I would like to acknowledge the courage of the four women who shared their struggles with dyslexia. It is my hope that the telling of their struggles will inform the parents of today and tomorrow about the challenges facing their daughters with dyslexia.

To Dr. Mary Ariail, I owe my understanding of identities and the research process. I extend special gratitude to the women who each guided my work from their specialty areas. Dr. Amy Flint, Dr. Patricia Carter, and Dr. Dana Fox have placed their unique marks on my identity as an author. With their support, my journey was rich and meaningful, and this work more robust.

Many thanks and appreciation is also given to my children. Zac Hurst, Michelle Quick Hurst, Liz Hurst, and Brent Ruth have provided constant love and encouragement to this venture. My oldest son, Dr. Eric Hurst, has provided unique support as my mentor. To have a child as a mentor is a unique and wonderful experience. Finally, to my husband, Michael, I give thanks for his love, legal expertise, and willingness to support my work.

Library of Congress Cataloging-in-Publication Data

Hurst, Ellen Burns.
  Why can't my daughter read? : success strategies for helping girls with dyslexia and reading
difficulties / by Ellen Burns Hurst, Ph.D.
      pages cm
  Includes bibliographical references.
  ISBN 978-1-61821-025-8 (pbk.)
  1. Reading disability--United States. 2. Dyslexia. 3. Girls--Education--United States.
  4. Girls--Books and reading--United States. I. Title.
  LB1050.5.H87 2012
  371.91'44--dc23

                              2012039422

Edited by Lacy Compton

Cover and layout design by Raquel Trevino

ISBN-13: 978-1-61821-025-8

At the time of this book's publication, all facts and figures cited are the most current available. All telephone numbers, addresses, and websites URLs are accurate and active. All publications, organizations, websites, and other resources exist as described in the book, and all have been verified. The author and Prufrock Press Inc. make no warranty or guarantee concerning the information and materials given out by organizations or content found at websites, and we are not responsible for any changes that occur after this book's publication. If you find an error, please contact Prufrock Press Inc.

Prufrock Press Inc.
P.O. Box 8813
Waco, TX 76714-8813
Phone: (800) 998-2208
Fax: (800) 240-0333
http://www.prufrock.com

Table of Contents

CHAPTER 1

Why My Daughter?

Once upon a time, there lived a beautiful prom queen. This prom queen possessed all of the requisite physical characteristics that one might expect in a fantasy queen. She had golden tresses, blue eyes, porcelain skin, and a perfect white smile. She gave the illusion of developed sexuality without denying the possibility of innocence. She was a combination of loner and outsider. She had the genius of communication. She could be characterized as a cultural heroine in that she unified the individual and the group. However, our prom queen differs significantly in one aspect of her life—she lived with a secret that she kept hidden throughout her school years. This young woman walked into my office and set this book into motion. This vision of perfection had one veiled flaw. She could not read.

As much as 15%–20% of the population demonstrates a significant reading disability (National Institute of Child Health and Human Development [NICHD], 2000). This means that 4 or 5 children in the average classroom will have some form of reading disability. The symptoms of this disability may include slow or inaccurate reading, poor spelling, poor writing, or difficulty with comprehension. Whether these individuals qualify for special educational services is uncertain, but what is certain is that they are likely to struggle with many aspects of the learning process.

The fundamental and powerful assumptions of our culture regarding literacy are that it is inherently good for the individual, good for the culture, difficult to acquire, and should be transmitted in classrooms. If literacy is difficult to acquire, then it becomes necessary to create a multitude of reasons to explain why some read better than others, as well as the cultural imperative to label as inferior those individuals who have poor reading skills. The consequence of believing that literacy is best learned in classrooms enables schools to create a monopoly in which they blindly repeat the same failed instructional practices with the expectation of a different outcome.

A history of learning disabilities (LD) in the United States reveals much about the cultural roles of literacy. After decades of neurological speculation regarding the exact nature of dyslexia, critics of the diagnosis of dyslexia still assert that it is nothing more than a plausible explanation of why children of privilege and intelligence do not learn to read as expected or a means of securing more time for labeled children on high stakes examinations (Elliott & Gibbs, 2008). However, the breakthrough of neuroimaging in children with dyslexia has revealed scientific evidence that individuals with dyslexia have a reduced engagement of the left temporo-parietal cortex for phonological processing of print (Shaywitz, 2003). This same neuroimaging technique confirms the plasticity of the brain as it responds to effective intervention. Behavioral and brain measures identify infants and young children at risk for dyslexia. Subsequent procedures demonstrate that preventive intervention is often effective and document the plasticity of the brain. There is hope that a combination of targeted teaching practices and cognitive neuroscience measures could prevent dyslexia from occurring in the majority of children who would otherwise develop dyslexia. To fully explore this phenomenon, it is necessary to understand the complexity of dyslexia.

The difficulties and concerns of a parent advocating for the child with reading disabilities are already significant. The confusion and misconceptions surrounding the diagnosis and treatment of dyslexia only add to the parental dilemma. Unfortunately, there are charlatans who will take emotional and financial advantage of the desperate parents of the reading disabled. Providers of costly vision therapy require parents to commit to 60–90 hours of left-to-right tracking exercises at \$90–\$120 an hour. Trendy movement therapy promises improved balance in the body and the brain. The neighborhood chiropractor is more than willing to lead the dyslexic child through a series of exercises promised to improve reading performance. Strip mall learning centers often charge high rates for computer-based instruction that is monitored by rotating tutors with questionable credentials. The well-meaning but misinformed reading specialist assures the parents that their child's reading will improve if only they use multicolored overlays on the child's reading materials.

The correction of this very serious disability is not so simple. In order to seriously address the identification and remediation of dyslexic children, and protect the parents of these children from unnecessary expenditure of time and money, the myths and misconceptions surrounding dyslexia must be addressed. As we work to deconstruct the masculinized educational framework in an attempt to make the system more equitable, often forgotten are the compliant girls who are experiencing academic difficulty. The gender normative behavior of boys demands most of the attention of teachers and administrators. As a reading specialist working primarily with diagnosed dyslexics, I am acutely aware that the immediate and long-term impact of dyslexia upon the lives of girls is only now beginning to be considered.

Literacy and Identity

Literacy goes far beyond a set of reading and writing skills. We should consider literacy identity as being an integral part of our daughters' evolving personal identity. Each girl's literacy identity determines what she chooses to read and what she chooses to read becomes an integral part of who she thinks she is. Literacy goes to the heart of girls' motivations and aspirations for what they want to be. Recognizing literacy practices as social artifacts suggests that girls' identities mediate and are mediated by the texts they read, write, and talk about (Moje & Luke, 2009).

Given that identities are social rather than individual constructions, girls attach greater importance to their memberships in some social groups than they do to others. To gain entrance to the desired groups, they seek out or avoid certain practices of literacy. Each girl has the option of participating or not participating in the literacy practices of the distinct groups to which they aspire to belong. Identity is in play in all of these social interactions. This is especially true in classroom interactions.

Teachers play a significant role in the creation of our daughters' identities. Literacy and identity are interdependent, so a girl's ability to progress and change is helped or hindered by her access or lack of access to a variety of literacy opportunities. The teacher controls these opportunities.

Many undiagnosed dyslexic girls enter the "closet" early in life, spending their childhood years anxiously avoiding classroom participation in oral reading for fear of embarrassment and disclosure. Disclosure would be social suicide and, as such, access to group affiliations would be limited. Girls tend to be affiliative by nature (Gilligan, 1982). They value those who are friendly, sociable, helpful, skillful in dealing with people, and open about their feelings. The fear of possible peer rejection that would result from public disclosure of poor literacy skills results in sustained levels of anxiety. Carried further, this fear of disclosure and possible peer rejection may curtail participation in typical literacy activities such as note writing, e-mailing, blogging, journaling, and yearbook signing.

A partial explanation for the decline in girls' self-perceptions may lie in the ways girls' classroom roles are constructed. From years of research and data gathered in hundreds of classroom interactions, Sadker and Sadker (1994) concluded that teachers often engage in inadvertent yet insidious forms of sexual discrimination that marginalize girls and limit the ways girls may see themselves. Teachers often encourage girls to take on identities that emphasize nurturing, such as mother or teacher, and although these identities may provide girls with increased power in some classroom relations, they also deny girls access to other roles. Language arts, perhaps more than any other academic discipline, has the potential to facilitate identity development. The nature of the literacy curriculum inherently lends itself to the exploration of identities, focused as it is on individuals' abilities to read, write, listen, and speak.

The position of power that each classroom teacher holds requires that we take an even closer look at the philosophical and academic profiles of the teachers with whom we entrust the academic and social growth of our girls. The majority of teachers in today's workforce are White, female, and middle class. Teachers of color comprise about 16% of the teaching force in the United States (Banks et al., 2005). As an adjunct professor in a Research I university, I am aware that undergraduate and graduate students are receiving their literacy coursework from professors who refuse to move on from whole language methodology. First, they feel morally bound to the constructivist philosophy of whole language instruction despite research to the contrary. Secondly, they have limited knowledge of linguistics-based instruction. In addition to limited university training, preservice as well as in-service teachers have little experience with children with learning differences or those from cultures and languages different from their own.

It is essential to understand that domination and elitism born in America's universities still exists in America's classrooms in order to fully understand how the literacy identity in dyslexic girls occurs. As Griffiths (1995) noted:

> Feminism is not just theoretically significant. Educational practices and educational outcomes are damaged by sexism. This is because there is a prevailing sexism both in and out of formal educational institutions: schools, universities, local authorities, governing bodies, government departments, educational publishing, and voluntary pressure groups. Inevitably sexism also distorts how such educational practices and outcomes are understood and researched. This is precisely the concern of feminist epistemology: how to improve knowledge and remove sexist distortions. (p. 219)

The significance of a compliant female with reading problems is far down the list of educational concerns. Historically, much of the focus of policy, practice, and research on gender and education has been on issues related to boys. The tide shifted in the 1990s with the publication of a number of reports and popular books about girls and their educational disadvantages. The American Association of University Women (AAUW, 1992) published the much-touted report *How Schools Shortchange Girls*, which focused on the argument that current curricula and pedagogy are educationally depriving girls. In addition, books such as *Failing at Fairness: How Our Schools Cheat Girls* (Sadker & Sadker, 1994), *Schoolgirls: Young Women, Self-Esteem, and the Confidence Gap* (Orenstein, 1994), and *Reviving Ophelia: Saving the Selves of Adolescent Girls* (Pipher, 2005), addressed the psychological damage and educational neglect to which girls are subjected in the male-dominated classroom. According to these authors, girls are called on less often by teachers, show less involvement and achievement in math and science, and receive fewer and lower quality comments from teachers.

Definitions

Nature of Dyslexia

Throughout the world there is a lack of consensus regarding the exact nature of dyslexia. The Dyslexia Society of Singapore (2009) defined dyslexia as a specific difficulty in reading, writing, and spelling. It asserted that dyslexia is not caused by a lack of intelligence or a lack of opportunity to learn. The National Center for Learning Disabilities (2012) asserted that dyslexia is a neurological disorder that causes children to process the information they read differently. It is described as a disability that persists across the lifespan of the individual. In addition, the individual's difficulties with phonological processing, rapid naming, working memory, processing speed, and the automatic development of skills are unexpected in relation to other cognitive abilities. Experts agree that dyslexia results in a pronounced difficulty in the ability to read and write. Yet, a precise description of the behavioral manifestations of this reading disability does not exist. The International Dyslexia Association (IDA) resolved one aspect of the confusion by establishing a broad-based definition of dyslexia. IDA (2002) defined dyslexia as follows:

> Dyslexia is a specific learning disability that is neuro-logical in origin. It is characterized by difficulties with accurate and/or fluent word recognition and by poor spelling and decoding abilities. These difficulties typi-cally result from a deficit in the phonological compo-nent of language that is often unexpected in relation to other cognitive abilities and the provision of effec-tive classroom instruction. Secondary consequences may include problems in reading comprehension and reduced reading experience that can impede growth of vocabulary and background knowledge. (p. 2)

The IDA definition is vague relative to the issue of the neuro-logical origins of dyslexia. The definition minimizes the possibility that gender, race, class, and instructional practices could contribute to or exacerbate the propensity for developing this condition. Frith (1999) stated that in order to fully understand dyslexia we need to link together cultural, biological, and behavioral factors. He contended that we must consider the possibility that these three factors alone or in concert can aggravate or ameliorate the condition.

The work of Dr. Sally Shaywitz (2003) resulted in a new definition of dyslexia based on neuroimaging studies of dyslexics. Technological advances in the form of functional MRIs substantiate the view that dyslexia is a neurodevelopmental disorder with a biological origin. The future holds new avenues for research in the area of dyslexia. The continued discussion of neuroimaging and brain-based research holds great promise. The possibility that a specific gene can be identified to explain the genetic component of dyslexia opens new opportuni-ties for research and cure (Nöthen et al., 1999). We are still a long way from understanding the causes of reading deficiencies. There is hope that with the collaboration between neuroscience, psychology, and education, we will be able to expand our understanding of dyslexia. As we explore these new avenues for research, it is important that those who suffer from dyslexia and their advocates continue to educate themselves regarding the facts about dyslexia.

Dyslexia Misconceptions

Many misconceptions (see Table 1) concerning the definition of dyslexia exist. In order to delve into the social construction and the biological origins of dyslexia, it is imperative that these misconceptions be replaced with accurate facts. The most common misconception concerning dyslexia is that it can be diagnosed when a student writes letters or words backward (Shaywitz, 2003). Teachers and parents become overly concerned when they see evidence of these reversals in the writing samples of children. Badian (2005) reported that reversal errors are likely to disappear in children with reading disabilities as their reading and writing skills improve. The observation of reversals is not unique to the reading and writing of struggling readers. During the developmental process of acquiring literacy, most children engage in some level of word and letter reversals before the age of 8. Shaywitz (2003) asserted that there is no evidence that dyslexics actually see letters and words backward. The core of dyslexia is not visual perception. The basis of dyslexia is a problem with processing language at the phoneme level. Kutz (1997) explained that phonemes are the representation of sounds that are meaningful within a language. These sounds allow individuals to distinguish one word from another. Thus, the deficiency in the dyslexic is the inability to distinguish the phonemic difference between /big/ and /pig/ rather than the ability to distinguish the graphic differences of the letters. Shaywitz (2003) expressed concern that many children will not be correctly diagnosed because they do not make the stereotypical reversals.

The assumption that dyslexia is the result of a visual processing deficit leads to a second common misconception. The use of colored text overlays or lenses is purported to be the quick fix for reading disabilities by those who believe in this misconception. Stone and Harris

Table 1

Myths and Misconceptions About Dyslexia

Myths	Facts
Dyslexia can be diagnosed when a student writes letters or words backward.	▪ Shaywitz (2003) asserted that there is no evidence that dyslexics actually see letters and words backward. ▪ The deficiency in the dyslexic is the inability to distinguish the phonemic difference between /big/ and /pig/ rather than the ability to distinguish the graphic differences of the letters. ▪ Many children will not be correctly diagnosed because they do not make reversals.
The use of colored text overlays or lenses is a quick fix.	▪ There is no substantive research that supports this theory. ▪ "Vision therapy" is not recognized by the American Academy of Ophthalmology as a treatment for reading disabilities.
Dyslexia affects more boys than girls.	▪ Shaywitz (2003) gave evidence that as many girls are affected by dyslexia as are boys. ▪ Gender specific behavior of boys is misinterpreted as a symptom of a learning disability. ▪ Many girls go undiagnosed because of absence of behaviors that disturb instruction.
Dyslexia only affects people who speak English.	▪ Dyslexia occurs cross-culturally, even in languages and cultures that do not use an alphabetic script. ▪ Dyslexic Chinese readers are described as having a rapid-naming deficit and an orthographic deficit (Ho, Chan, Leung, Lee, & Sang, 2005).
Dyslexics can never learn to read.	▪ Recent imaging studies reveal that those individuals who receive appropriate intense instruction can learn to read. ▪ Images obtained from functional MRIs after this intervention show the emergence of brain pathways comparable to those of good readers. ▪ The nature of this instruction must address the difficulty the child is having with phonemic processing. ▪ Instruction must remediate phonological weaknesses and access higher level thinking skills through curriculum and learning accommodations.

Table 1, continued

Myths	Facts
Dyslexia can be fixed or solved easily.	■ There are those who will take emotional and financial advantage of the desperate parents of the reading disabled. ■ Vision therapists assert that 60–90 hours of left-to-right tracking exercises at $90–$120 an hour will solve the problem. Learning centers charge high prices for computer-based tutoring monitored by often unqualified reading tutors. ■ Dyslexia has become big business that preys on the desperate and the affluent.

(1991) reviewed evidence for the existence of scotopic sensitivity syndrome (SSS). SSS allegedly is manifested as a visual disturbance related to light. Treatment for SSS includes the wearing of colored glasses or the use of colored plastic sheet overlays on reading materials. Stone and Harris asserted that the diagnosis of this condition is extremely subjective and raises questions of accuracy and reliability of previous studies.

Early studies reinforced the third misconception—that dyslexia affects more boys than girls. Gaub and Carlson (1997) suggested that the girls who are referred to clinics are those most severely affected. They trigger the referral process as a result of the "squeaking wheel" phenomenon by displaying co-occurring overt behavioral patterns of inattention. Szatmari's (1992) population studies found a ratio of identification of one girl for every three male diagnoses. However, Shaywitz (2003) gave evidence that as many girls are affected by dyslexia as are boys. She suggested that the reason that the overidentification of boys occurs is the manifestation of gender specific behavior. The occurrence of hyperactive and impulsive behavior by dyslexic boys is reported at a higher rate than that exhibited by dyslexic girls. The result is a disproportional referral rate. This argument presupposes a gender difference in the activity levels of boys and girls. When girls display behaviors that mirror that of aggressive male behavior, it triggers the referral process and the subsequent diagnosis of a reading disability.

Parents are not the only group struggling to make sense out of this difficult problem. Among the misinformed are educators who substitute multicolored overlays on the child's reading materials for appropriate corrective instruction or assume that the girls in their class are good readers. The treatment of this very serious disability is complex. Educators must address the problems of identification and remediation of dyslexic children. They must inform and protect the parents of these children so they are able to avoid unnecessary expenditures of time and money.

Recognizing Reading Difficulties

I grew up on a farm, which was the best thing that ever happened. But when I was 5 and moved to Lynchburg, VA, I entered kindergarten for the first time and don't remember anything remarkable about that at all. I changed schools in the first grade and I remember having trouble with some pronunciations. By the time I was in the third grade and reading Dick, Jane, and Sally with my father at night, anything that started in a WH I couldn't figure it out. Had no idea. I couldn't do a what, when, why, where. I can do that now. I couldn't do it in the third grade and my father could not figure it out—in his words, "Honey, what the hell is wrong with you?" My mother, oddly enough, was a kindergarten teacher. So, she saw that I was having some trouble reading, and she encouraged me to read. But I didn't like it. It was a chore. Really hard. And if you had told me what I'd read I couldn't possibly tell you. Had no retention. None. So then she decided I needed piano lessons, like I could read those notes and I couldn't read Dick, Jane, and Sally? What I remember particularly about learning

> to play the piano was that if you would play it for me,
> I could pick out the notes with my fingers. If I could
> hear it, I could learn it. And taking piano lessons was
> the first time I realized if you would read it to me, I
> could get it. —Lucy

My years of working as a reading specialist have been filled with conversations with parents in which they report they have been told that their daughter's reading delay was due to nothing more than a developmental lag. They are told to give it some time, and their daughter will eventually catch up. When a kindergartener confuses letters, associates the wrong sound with a letter, or cannot distinguish a rhyme, it usually has nothing to do with social maturity. Please do not accept the developmental lag excuse. If your intuition tells you something is not right, do not wait to seek help.

NICHD (2000) stated that 59% of poor readers can be brought up to grade level if they receive appropriate early intervention. Of course, it is still possible to help an older child with reading, but children beyond third grade require much more frequent and intensive help. The longer you wait to get help for a child with reading difficulties, the harder it will be for the child to catch up. Seventy-five percent of children receiving intervention at age 9 or later continue to struggle throughout their school careers. Waiting until fourth grade, rather than taking action in kindergarten, will only make the task of remediation more complex and time intensive. It will take four times as long to obtain equivalent results. Awareness of the red flags of a reading disability is the first step to an early and accurate diagnosis (see Table 2).

Because of these red flags, it is imperative for schools to implement systematic screening plans. The best plan is to begin screening children in early kindergarten and continue screening at least three times a year until the end of third grade. The rationale is that it is better to slightly overidentify the number of children who may be at risk of reading difficulty than to miss some who may need help. The worst outcome of overidentification is that a child who would eventually have caught on receives some additional help.

Table 2

Red Flags of Reading Disorders

Grade	Red Flag
Pre–K/ Kindergarten (Kaufman & Hook, 1996)	▪ Delay in talking ▪ Difficulty recognizing and producing rhymes ▪ Difficulty remembering rote information, such as letter names ▪ Difficulty remembering or following directions
Grades 1–3	▪ Difficulty with sound/symbol correspondence (/a/, as in apple) ▪ Confusion with letters that look alike (b/d/p, w/m, h/n, f/t) ▪ Confusion with letters that have similar sounds (d/t, b/p, f/v) ▪ Difficulty remembering common sight words (was, the, and, she) ▪ Problems segmenting words into sounds (cat is /k/ /a/ /t/) ▪ Difficulty blending individual sounds to make words ▪ Reading and spelling errors that indicate difficulty sequencing sounds (blast becomes blats) ▪ Omission of grammatical endings when reading and writing (-s, -ed, -ing) ▪ Difficulty remembering spelling of words over time ▪ Slow rate of letter, object, and number naming
Grades 4–8	▪ Significant difficulty reading and spelling multisyllabic/longer words (e.g., omits whole syllables) ▪ Reduced awareness of word structure (prefix, roots, and suffixes) ▪ Frequent misreading of common sight words ▪ Difficulty learning new information from text because of word reading errors ▪ Difficulty understanding text because of underlying oral language problems with vocabulary and/or grammar ▪ Significant difficulty writing, due to spelling and organization problems ▪ Slow rate of reading

Table 2, continued

Grade	Red Flag
Grades 9–12, Adults	• Continued difficulty with word recognition that significantly affects acquisition of knowledge and ability to analyze written material • Slow rate of reading • Continued difficulty with spelling and written composition • Difficulty taking notes in class • Trouble learning a foreign language

Parenting a Child Who Struggles With Reading

In first grade, Trisha sat in a circle with the other kids. They were all holding *Our Neighborhood*, their first reader, sounding out letters and words. They said, "Beh, beh . . . oy, boy, and luh, luh . . . ook, look." The teacher smiled at them when they put all the sounds together and got a word right. But when Trisha looked at a page, all she saw were wiggling shapes, and when she tried to sound out words, the other kids laughed at her. "Trisha, what are you looking at in that book?" they'd say. "I'm reading!" she'd say back to them. But her teacher would move on to the next person. Always when it was her turn to read, her teacher had to help her with every single word. And while the other kids moved up into the second reader and third reader, she stayed alone in *Our Neighborhood*. Trisha began to feel "different." She began to feel dumb. (Polacco, 1998, p. 22)

Conventional wisdom would have parents believe that their daughter will learn to read naturally if they surround her with books and copious oral reading from an early age. Parents doing all of the "right things" are devastated when their normal, intelligent daughter is not an early reader. Not all children come into kindergarten as readers or knowing all of their letters. As kindergarten draws to a close, some of the children will have significant difficulty with reading if they do not receive the right kind of reading instruction. Most children must be taught *how* to read, even though they love the books and stories the adults in their lives share with them.

Programmatic research over the past 35 years has not supported the view that reading development reflects a natural process—that girls learn to read as they learn to speak, through natural exposure to a literate environment. To the contrary, certain aspects of learning to read are highly unnatural. The process of isolating phonemes from speech and associating them to letters and letter patterns is unlike any process in the child's linguistic repertoire. Unlike learning to speak, beginning readers must appreciate consciously what the symbols stand for in the writing system they learn (Lieberman, 1992). The English alphabetic symbols are arbitrary and abstract. If learning to read were natural, why does our society have so many youngsters and adults who are illiterate?

Despite strong evidence to the contrary, many educators and researchers maintain the perspective that reading is an almost instinctive, natural process. They believe that explicit instruction in phonemic awareness, phonics, structural analysis, and reading comprehension strategies is unnecessary because oral language skills provide the reader with a meaning-based structure for the decoding and recognition of unfamiliar words (Edelsky, Altweger, & Flores, 1991; Goodman 1996).

Scientific research, however, simply does not support the claim that meaningful context and authentic text alone are sufficient for the development of decoding skills. Reliance on linguistic context requires the child to guess the pronunciation of words from context. This is based on the assumption that the textual context provides all of the clues necessary for accurate and consistent predictions. But content-specific words found in the typical elementary content-area texts—the concept-laden words necessary for text comprehension—can be predicted from surrounding context only 10%–20% of the time (Gough,

Alford, & Holley-Wilcox, 1981). Rather than relying on context, beginning readers must be taught a consistent system to decode letters to sounds through research-based, sequential, complete, and accurate instruction.

How Do Children Learn to Read English?

Reading is the product of decoding and comprehension (Gough et al., 1981). Although this sounds simple, learning to read is much tougher than people think. To learn to decode and read printed English, children must be aware that spoken words are composed of individual sound parts called phonemes. This is what is meant by *phonemic awareness*.

Phonemic awareness and phonics are not the same. When educators assess phonemic awareness skills, they ask children to demonstrate knowledge of the sound structure of words *without any letters or written words present*. For example, "What word would be left if the /k/ sound were taken away from cat?" or "What sounds do you hear in the word big?" To assess phonics skills, they ask children to link sounds (phonemes) with letters. Thus, the development of phonics skills depends on the development of phonemic awareness.

Phonemic awareness is critical in beginning reading because to read an alphabetic language like English, children must know that written spellings systematically represent spoken sounds. When youngsters figure this out, either on their own or with direct instruction, they have acquired the alphabetic principle. However, if beginning readers have difficulty perceiving the sounds in spoken words—for example, if they cannot "hear" the /at/ sound in *fat* and *cat* and perceive that the difference lies in the first sound—they will have difficulty decoding or sounding out new words. In turn, developing reading fluency will be difficult, resulting in poor comprehension, limited learning, and little enjoyment.

We are beginning to understand why many children have difficulty developing phonemic awareness. When we speak to one another, the individual sounds (phonemes) within the words are not consciously heard by the listener. Thus, no one ever receives any "natural" practice understanding that words are composed of smaller, abstract sound units. For example, when one utters the word "bag," the ear hears only one sound, not three (as in /b/ /a/ /g/). This is because when "bag" is spoken, the /a/ and /g/ phonemes are folded into the initial /b/ sound. Thus, the acoustic information presented to the ears reflects an overlapping bundle of sound, not three discrete sounds. This process ensures rapid, efficient communication. Consider the time it would take to have a conversation if each of the words we uttered were segmented into their underlying sound structures.

However, nature has provided a conundrum here: What is good for the listener is not so good for the beginning reader. Although spoken language is seamless, the beginning reader must detect the seams in speech, unglue the sounds from one another, and learn which sounds (phonemes) go with which letters. We now understand that specific systems in the brain recover sounds from spoken words, and just as in learning any skill, children understand phonemic awareness with different aptitudes and experiences.

Reading ability is like height and weight: It is distributed on a continuum. Some people are very good at it, some people are very poor at it, and the rest are somewhere in between. In this way, reading ability is like musical ability, athletic ability, artistic talent, and mathematical ability. Reading ability, however, is *not* just a reflection of intelligence. Some very intelligent children have trouble reading, and some decidedly unintelligent children can read fairly well. For children who have very few other problems, reading might not "click" and spelling might be well-nigh impossible.

In my years as a reading specialist, I have worked with a multitude of bright children who experienced difficulty with reading. I have worked with hundreds of parents who have documented the problems they have encountered as they sought help for their struggling readers. When reading is hard for one of your children, you may feel uncertain, anxious, confused, helpless, and angry.

Parents often share their shame over their inability to act sooner when they sensed that something was wrong. Many wish that they had known more about learning to read so that they could have made better choices or understood what their child was facing. In hindsight, they wish they had questioned the teacher's judgment and trusted their own.

The reasons parents hesitate to question school personnel or express their concerns vary. Most often, respect for the authority of teachers and doubts about their own knowledge of the reading process inhibit parental action. The act of challenging school authority based on intuition rather than substantive knowledge is a daunting process. We want to believe that educators can be trusted to meet our children's needs, yet often the parent is the first or only adult to recognize a child's learning problem. The act of questioning teachers or administrators constitutes an act of intrusion or crossing an important boundary. Teachers forced to answer difficult questions sense that their territory is being violated. The stakes are too high to avoid the crossing of this territorial barrier. Before taking the difficult first step on the journey to help your daughter, you must be armed with information and the determination to be undaunted by the many roadblocks you may face. Parents who understand the risks of delay in getting help for their daughters' reading problems are motivated not to wait. Children can be brought up to grade level much more successfully and with less effort if effective intervention is offered early on.

About This Book

After years of working with students who stuggle with the burden of low literacy skills, it is my hope that the chapters to come will inform and enpower you.

In Chapter 2: The Risks of Waiting: Why We Can't Ignore Girls' Reading Struggles, you are asked to wrap your head around the outcomes of failing to diagnose dyslexia in girls. Throughout the chapter, I provide insights into true stories of how undiagnosed girls with dyslexia negotiated school with undeveloped literacy skills.

The processes girls use to disguise their reading difficulties are deconstructed in Chapter 3: Shame and Passing as Literate. Goffman (1959) asserted that people select fronts that are considered socially acceptable and that represent aspects of an ideal identity. Goffman referred to "passing" and "management" activities as the means by which fronts are maintained. Individuals attempt to pass as having a particular identity. This task requires expert management of the contexts around them. Through the construction of elaborate scenes, they provide support to the front identity. One problem for the undiagnosed dyslexic reader is that maintaining the front of literacy expert may take up so much energy that there is little opportunity or energy left to learn to read.

In Chapter 4: Taking Action Before Dyslexia and Identity Collide, we will explore how girls figure out the parts of their world they will enter temporarily or peripherally and those they will enter with positions of power and prestige. For some, positions are predetermined culturally and socially. This is especially true in the schools of the United States. Girls who have difficulty with literacy skills are positioned as "struggling" (Ash, 2002), "remedial" (Wilhelm, 1997), "reluctant" (Wilhelm, 1997), and "marginalized" (Moje, Young, Readence, & Moore, 2000). Thus, undiagnosed dyslexic girls, through the marginalizing labels we place upon them, are often set up to become resistant to reading. As Alvermann (2001b) so aptly stated, "Culture constructs disability, as well as ability" (p. 677).

Chapter 5: Dyslexia vs. Dysteachia discusses the disturbing fact that the professionals from whom you seek help for your struggling daughter may not have the skills or knowledge to provide the help you so desperately need. Faced with this realization, you must arm yourself with the information to both teach and advocate for your daughter.

This leads you to Chapter 6: What Parents Can Do At Home to Increase Reading Abilities. Here you will find the nuts and bolts of reading intervention for all aspects of the reading process. In addition, suggestions for the use of technology to improve reading skills are provided.

The last chapter is your guide to advocacy. I hope that you are in a situation in which you are working as a partner with your daughter's school to improve her performance. If that is not the case, Chapter 7: Becoming Your Daughter's Advocate will give you an overview of your legal rights as well as links to more in-depth legal expertise. As you read the last chapter, I hope you feel inspired and informed. I know how difficult your journey is. I applaud all you have already done to help your daughter and all that you will do in the future.

Conclusion

We have just begun the journey to acquire the necessary knowledge to empower you as a true advocate for your daughter. We have seen that girls historically have been ignored in the public schools of the United States. In addition, their literacy identities have been squelched because of limited opportunities. We have delved into the nature of dyslexia and are now aware of those misconceptions that can lead us down the wrong path. Next we will see the urgency of early intervention and the disastrous effect of waiting too long to take action.

CHAPTER 2

The Risks of Waiting
Why We Can't Ignore Girls' Reading Struggles

There's no doubt that as a parent of a daughter who struggles to read, you want to find solutions that will help her begin to succeed. However, some parents may dismiss smaller struggles early in a girl's life, not realizing the tremendous impact early intervention can have. In order to emphasize the risks of waiting to provide early interventions for girls with reading difficulties, I will share the retrospective stories of three girls and their struggle with undiagnosed dyslexia: Lucy, Susie, and Molly. Their voices will tell of their journey with dyslexia and share insights into how waiting to intervene can cause significant problems for girls.

Throughout the chapter, I provide explanations of their stories to provide a deeper understanding of how undiagnosed dyslexic girls negotiate school. The actual words of the girls are used whenever possible. To achieve this end, each girl will be introduced, the nature of her school experiences will be examined, and finally, the diversionary behaviors and strategies associated with the act of appearing to be literate will be analyzed.

Lucy

Lucy Negotiates Reading

Lucy grew up on a farm, which she said "was the best thing that ever happened" to her. When she was 5, she moved to Lynchburg, VA, and entered kindergarten, the first of several moves during her early years. Her first memories of difficulty with the reading process were triggered by memories of her third move. When she changed schools in the first grade, she remembers having trouble with "some pronunciations."

Lucy's literacy journey took a detour when she encountered her first basal reader around third grade. The texts used a controlled vocabulary and phonics method. Millions of children have learned to read through these basal-style textbooks. Unfortunately, Lucy was not one of them.

Lucy Negotiates Family

Lucy's mother, a kindergarten teacher, recognized that Lucy struggled with reading. She encouraged Lucy to read, but she met strong resistance. Lucy already perceived reading as a chore. When Lucy did acquiesce and engage in reading practice, she had no retention of what she had read, thus feeding the cycle of frustration and resistance. Even as an educator, Lucy's mother lacked the information that might enable her to attain insights into her daughter's condition. Frustrated, Lucy's mother enrolled her in a speed reading course, which added to everyone's frustration:

> We didn't know about it then. We just didn't know about it. You know, they didn't know much about dyslexia. Mother, bless her heart, one summer sent me to a speed reading class. (Laughter) I'd get so . . . frustrated.

When speed reading proved to be ineffective, Lucy's mother attempted a new tactic. She enrolled Lucy in piano lessons. Lucy's reaction to this new challenge was bittersweet. The task of learning to read music mocked her weakness, but the music itself provided Lucy with her first glimpse of her innate potential to learn: "If I could hear it I could learn it. And taking piano lessons was the first time I realized if you would read it to me, I could get it."

Lucy was the firstborn child. She had a brother who was just a year and 8 days younger than she. He carried her father's name, and he looked like her father. Not surprisingly, Lucy believed that he was the favored child. Rather than being an ally, her brother added to the growing throng of those who made Lucy feel inferior. As she recalls the influence of her brother on her life, enmeshed in her words are signals that reveal the birth of resistance to her positioning as "poor Lucy" and hints of emerging agency.

> My brother always tried to make me feel like I was dumb. "Aww, sis," he'd say. It was his favorite expression. "Aww, sis, you can't figure out anything." And the truth was I could figure out a lot of things. I had huge street sense. I mean, I could find my way around a strange city because I knew north, south, east, and west. Or I'd listen to the news, and I could tell you what happened at the White House the day before.

Familial expectations could have solidified Lucy's positioning as one with little academic ability. Her words suggest that she had fallen prey to the labels placed on her by the individuals in her life. Yet, she subtly reveals a growing disassociation with this powerless positioning when she refers to herself in the third person and expresses growing discontent with the position to which she has been recruited.

> So Lucy was always a C student and just happened to have a brother with a 158 IQ. Lucy brought home Cs, but if her brother brought home one B he was grounded. He was the genius. I would hear my father

saying, "That's all poor Lucy can do." Lucy just got tired of being poor Lucy.

A particular strength of the poststructuralist perspective on identity is that it recognizes the essential force of discourse, the way one talks about the self, and at the same time recognizes that people are capable of exercising choice in relation to those discourses (Broughton & Fairbanks, 2002). One Saturday afternoon, Lucy's mother gave her the opportunity to experience the power of discourse. Lucy's mother escorted her into the kitchen and asked her to sit on a stool in the middle of the kitchen. From this position of physical isolation and emotional abandonment, Lucy faced a barrage of questions concerning her current schooling and her plans for the future. Lucy accepted this unexpected attention and immersed herself in a one-on-one session with her mother replete with harsh self-reflection and a subsequent rebirth. Through the course of the afternoon, she engaged in the process of assessing her strengths and weaknesses. To be Lucy, she must understand herself from the perspective of others while protecting herself from their grasps.

> I don't know how, um, it all happened but I knew that I couldn't read. I knew that I wasn't pretty. And I had to find a gimmick to get along. So I used whatever comedic skills I had, and when my mother put me on a bar stool one Saturday, she told me I wasn't getting up until I knew what I was going to do when I went to college. Now, I'd never expressed any burning desire to go to college, but she had gone to college and daddy had, so therefore, I was. So I sat there and I went through the professions, accountants and lawyers and doctors, and knew I didn't want to be in education because all I heard was that crap across the dining room table every night. Finally, it came to me. I said, "Mother, I've got it."
>
> She said, "What?"
>
> I said, "I want to be Lucille Ball."

And I knew it right then. I wanted to be Lucy. And I figured out that the more humorous I was, the further I got, and I didn't have to say a lot. I just had to observe and think and say something funny.

Once Lucy established her protective identity as Lucille Ball, she was able to see the world from a new vantage point. At that moment, in terms of the images, metaphors, stories, and concepts that are now relevant, Lucy gained novel perspectives on the world through which she could learn to view peers, assets, limitations, and behaviors with new meaning. Her new position as Lucy provided her with the capacity to influence her own behavior in her world. Even with the new persona, Lucy still had to negotiate the issues surrounding her undiagnosed dyslexia and face the conflict caused by her relegation to groups designated for students with low reading ability.

Lucy Negotiates Stigma and Shame

Lucy's relegation to the lowest performing reading group in secondary school was excruciating. She recounted her first experience with ability grouping. Her final comments were words that revealed her continued resistance to the position of "poor Lucy," its concomitant stigma, and the power of her growing strength.

I was put in classes that had the slower, poorer students. I know that for a fact.

They were all the goobers around me, not the cool smart kids.

I didn't know it was coming until I realized that it had hit me. And then I went up to my teacher, who was single, and I said, "You know, Miss McCutcheon, I think you and I are the only two in here who aren't married." She burst out laughing. Because I knew I was in a class with a bunch of [kids she felt were less intelligent]. [pause] I knew more than those other kids somehow.

Donna Alvermann (2001b) suggested that our identities as readers are decided for us. As noted in Chapter 1, readers who have difficulty with literacy skills are positioned as "struggling" (Ash, 2002), "remedial" (Wilhelm, 1997), "reluctant" (Wilhelm, 1997), and "marginalized" (Moje, Young, Readence, & Moore, 2000), among other labels. Lucy was blindsided by her positioning as a struggling reader and used humor to negotiate the marginalizing label placed upon her. She reached out to her only intellectual equal in the room to seek acknowledgment that this classroom was not where she belonged.

Lucy Negotiates Peers

Despite Bourdieu and Passeron's (1990) assertions that our positions in society are coerced by societal pressures and are immutable, Lucy found cracks and openings that allowed her to take up positions as something other than those by which she was recognized in the social and cultural worlds she inhabited (Bettie, 2003). These cracks provided a space by which, in the ongoing interactions of her social and cultural lives, Lucy could act in ways that positioned her differently. In other words, they provided a space for agency or change.

Given that literacy shaming is a potent and debilitating form of symbolic violence (Bourdieu & Passeron, 1990), this type of denigration should have reflected negatively on Lucy's social standing and her ability to command peer respect. All human actions take place within social fields, which are the arenas in which the struggle for available resources occurs. Individuals, institutions, and other agents try to distinguish themselves from others and acquire capital which is useful or valuable. Because fields are dynamic, valued forms of social and cultural capital are also dynamic and arbitrary. Social capital is inherent in the structure of relations between and among actors in and out of school. Lucy is quick to explain the benefits that her natural leadership abilities, interpersonal skills, and linguistic facility provide. Her social abilities expanded her social capital (Bourdieu, 1986) enough to warrant her recruitment and repositioning (Holland, Lachicotte, Skinner, & Cain, 1998) into the center of the school's social context, despite her reading difficulties, a common coping strategy for girls with dyslexia.

Her words provide the social perspective to witness how she authors the world with intention.

> Socially I tend to be a clown. Everybody wanted me to be president of everything and I was still a C student. There was a reason. And the answer was I'd get the job done.

With few traditional literacy skills, Lucy used her social capital to get things done. She delegated responsibilities to group members and created a cohesive whole to accomplish a task. To access needed information that was in print, she would "get my daddy to read something for me." She would say, "Daddy, read up on this for me and he'd just tell me and then I had it." Lucy also used the social capital of others to accomplish those tasks she could not get done alone. She told of needing an artist for a project, so she picked the two peers who had the artistic skills. When she needed someone who would be able to sell tickets, she recruited the "cute ones." She explained, "Cute people can always sell more tickets than ugly people. It's just a given. Not that it's right, but it's a given. And just things like that to get the task done." Lucy learned to use others' strengths to hide her struggles.

The Rest of Lucy's Story

Lucy successfully negotiated her world of school by using her social capital and by relying on her learning strengths to circumvent her literacy limitations. Miracles continued when she took an aptitude test. Lucy describes the test as not being the "usual test." She described it as a test about gears. Test items involved visual/spatial manipulations during which she had to determine "if a gear went this way and it grabbed teeth this way which direction did it go?" This task was repeated and culminated in solving the puzzle at the end. The test required no reading.

> I got the highest score in the class. So my teacher called me in and said, "Lucy, I've looked into your

> academic record." . . . He said, "I see you're a C stu-
> dent." And I said, "Yep, that's all I can do." And he
> said, "I want you to know you got the highest grade
> in the class." I said, "You must have somebody else's
> paper." He said, "No, you understood all of that and
> some of the other kids just got zeroes. They couldn't
> figure anything out and all your answers were right.
> How did you do that?" And again I said I don't know.
> I'd never taken a test with gears before. I didn't know
> how I knew that. A girl that couldn't pass math or
> reading. How could I do those gears? And I don't
> know the answer to a lot of questions, how I can do
> something. I just know that after he told me that I
> wasn't stupid, that I was not stupid any more. It was
> the first time I ever thought that I wasn't "poor Lucy."

The implications of this scenario are significant not only to the changing identities of Lucy, but also to the lives of individuals yet unchanged due to the absence of early diagnosis of dyslexia. Early diagnostic testing should occur whenever there are discrepancies or inconsistencies in students' academic skills. Children who have reported having difficulty understanding information, following instructions, misinterpreting information, or using the term "dumb" as a self-descriptor should be evaluated. If an early diagnostic evaluation had been given, Lucy might have been identified as a gifted student with dyslexia. Silverman (2002) coined the term "visual-spatial learner" to describe children like Lucy who see the big picture, but who have difficulty with regular step-by-step learning. Her book, *Upside-Down Brilliance: The Visual Spatial Learner*, explained why traditional classroom teaching can be debilitating and included practical teaching techniques to help these children experience success.

Years later, Lucy obtained a definitive diagnosis of dyslexia. When asked how she felt about knowing the cause of her reading struggles, Lucy's response reveals that she processed the diagnosis with the same sense of humor she used to process all of the challenges of her life.

OK, I haven't been able to read, I'm a C student. That guy that tested me on those gears told me I wasn't dumb. I get my sixes and nines wrong, and I always have my right and my lefts wrong. When I found out, I just went, "Well you're just a," as I call it, "a lex-dyxic." [laughs]

Susie

Susie Negotiates Reading

Raised in a seemingly traditional family, Susie bore the wounds inflicted by those individuals she trusted the most, her family and her teachers.

I have visions of first grade reading groups. And just, I never could figure out what—why those kids could understand—or could get from the written page what I couldn't. Well, I mean, they could look at the page and say, "This says this," and I'm going, "Where? How does it say that?" And, you know, eventually, you know, figured out enough pieces so I could struggle through.

But it was also wiggly. You know, my reading was wiggly.

Paulson (2005) asserted that the eyes of persons with dyslexia do not move relentlessly forward but go backward at times, fixate on some words more than once, skip some words altogether, spend a small portion of time on some words and a large portion of time on others, and even examine different parts of different words. It would take further assessment to determine the exact cause of Susie's difficulty in moving her eyes continuously from left to right. It may be related to her level of fatigue associated with decoding difficulties or it could demonstrate inconsistencies of expenditures of effort relative to perceived task difficulty. As Susie moved her eyes away from the text, she reported that looking for clues in the pictures could help identify the words. Susie describes the distraction of picture clues when unable to decode the word "splash."

Susie:	"Splash." I remember that one specifically.
Ellen:	What do you remember about "splash"?
Susie:	Oh, just that was—I didn't know the word.
Ellen:	Who did you look to, or did you look up?
Susie:	Um, I think I just looked at the picture.
Ellen:	Why did you search the picture?
Susie:	For that word that I don't know.
Ellen:	Do you have any memories of insights that helped you read?
Susie:	The only one—the only one I can think of as an "aha" moment is my fifth-grade teacher just saying, "Just look at a section of the word." That was a big thing.
Ellen:	What would she tell you to do?
Susie:	"Look at the first syllable."
Ellen:	And no one had said that to you up until that point?
Susie:	If they did, I hadn't been attending.
Ellen:	Did you start practicing that?
Susie:	It helped. Isn't that amazing? (laughs)
Ellen:	What was your strategy up to this point?
Susie:	Guessing.
Ellen:	Guessing whole words.
Susie:	Yeah.
Ellen:	Had you memorized a lot of whole words?
Susie:	No, I was a good guesser.
Ellen:	How did you guess?
Susie:	Well, the shape of the word was a big thing.
Ellen:	The shape, the configuration of the word.
Susie:	Mm-hmm.
Ellen:	Did you use the initial sound?
Susie:	Oh, yes, I always did the initial sounds. And the end sounds.
Ellen:	And the shape of the word.
Susie:	Mm-hmm. And what went on in the middle, who knows . . .
Ellen:	And if it made sense to you, you would just keep right on going.

Susie:	Mm-hmm, yep.
Ellen:	Do you still do that to this day?
Susie:	Yep, I do.
Ellen:	So when you're reading books on your own and you don't have the pressure of reading out loud, it really doesn't matter as long as the story continues.
Susie:	You guessed it. Oh, I was so cute, and I wanted to do such a good job, and I was so eager, and I really, really, really wanted to do well.
Ellen:	And so what other strategies did you use to try to ensure that you could do well?
Susie:	Oh, the pictures. You know, those—those pictures were great in those books. And I listened really carefully, I think, to what the other kids said.

To Susie, negotiating text seems to require mastery of a serial and linear process. Examination of most texts reveals serially presented text with letters and words proceeding from left to right, with no overlap or backtracking. Just and Carpenter (1980) formulated the hypothesis that there is no appreciable lag between what is fixated, maintaining the gaze on text, and what is processed. If this hypothesis is correct, then when the reader looks at a word or object, he or she also processes cognitively for exactly as long as the recorded fixation. Instead of a serial data uploading model, eye movement research points to the reader searching for information to aid in the construction of meaning. This difference may be subtle, but it is important as it relates to Susie's difficulty getting beyond midpoint in a line of print. The exact cause of her difficulty in moving her eyes continuously from left to right may be related to search for meaning. This hypothesis is substantiated by Susie's eye movements away from the text desperately looking for picture clues that could have had an impact on meaning as well.

Susie Negotiates Family

Osman (1997) suggested that the presence of a child with dyslexia in the family has a profound influence on family dynamics. This influence extends to the social and emotional development of siblings. Adverse familial effects are more likely to occur when (a) there are only two children, one of whom has a disabling condition; (b) the children are the same sex and close in age; (c) the child without the problem is the eldest female in the family; and (d) parents cannot accept their child's learning disability.

In families with affected children, parents tend to expect more of the unaffected sibling. These expectations often focus on high academic achievement. Osman (1997) suggested the focus on high academic achievement reflects the need by parents for the unaffected sibling to compensate for the underachievement of the dyslexic child. Minuchin (1988) also found that parents expect the unaffected sibling to perform better at school or excel in extracurricular activities and suggests that families with dyslexic and nondyslexic siblings are characterized by higher levels of anxiety and family discord. Lardieri, Blacher, and Swanson (2000) found that families experiencing high levels of stress could be characterized by dysfunction or chaos.

Susie's family was unusual in that both Susie and her brother had dyslexia. Curiously, Susie's dyslexia was ignored. When her little brother's reading problem surfaced, he became the focus of her mother's attention. He was designated as the child with reading issues. Susie's attempts at self-advocating for assistance with her reading difficulties were often ignored.

Susie:	I tried to tell her, "I think I do that, too." "No, you don't. You're fine."
Ellen:	So she was just in total denial.
Susie:	Yes.
Ellen:	Because she just couldn't—because she didn't want to deal with it?
Susie:	Well, I think—well . . . Yeah, I think that's part of it, or, you know, I was doing fine enough.
Ellen:	What does "fine enough" mean?
Susie:	You know, I—I wasn't raising any flags for anybody or causing anybody trouble. But I think, you know, maybe being a girl—well, I don't know if that's easier or not, but—
Ellen:	What do you mean? Talk about that.
Susie:	I just—well, girls are nicer people.

The fact that Susie's mother chose to overlook her dyslexia and focus on her brother's dyslexia is supported by the research of Gaub and Carlson (1997). They proposed that girls who are referred to clinics are those most severely affected. They trigger the referral process as a result of the "squeaking wheel" phenomenon by displaying co-occurring overt behavioral patterns of inattention. Szatmari's (1992) population studies found a ratio of identification of one female diagnosis for every three male diagnoses. Susie attributes her mother's rejection of her condition as being motivated by gendered differences in behavior and perceived need. So Susie was left to her own devices. Careful not to overly demonize her parents, she clarified, "They were crummy parents, but I don't think they were evil; I just needed you to know that."

Susie Negotiates Stigma and Shame

Susie revealed her diagnosis of comorbid conditions of Attention Deficit/Hyperactivity Disorder (ADHD) and dyslexia. Mayes and Calhoun (2000) reported that learning disabilities, such as dyslexia, are the most commonly coexisting conditions with ADHD. The secondary characteristics of dyslexia and ADHD in girls can have a profound influence on their adolescent literacy experiences. These secondary characteristics can include low self-esteem, depression, demoralization, stress, and social skills deficit.

When faced with the manifestation of these coexisting conditions in reading groups, likely and unlikely heroes came to Susie's rescue. Teachers turn often to those students who possess embodied reading capital (Compton-Lilly, 2007) to provide needed assistance for students who struggle with reading. Students with reading capital are those whose words, mannerisms, and gestures fulfill school ideals by displaying an allegiance to school-sanctioned reading norms. They read the right books. They participate in norms for reading behavior, such as reading silently, decoding words, and answering questions about stories. Susie's teacher favored a male member of the group who possessed reading capital while reinforcing Susie's position as helpless, further emphasizing her inadequacy as a reader.

Ellen:	When you didn't know a word, was there some-body stepping in as hero?
Susie:	Well, the teacher did, yeah.
Ellen:	If you didn't know a word, would she always sup-ply it? Do you recall?
Susie:	(pause) Yeah, and I think she would also encour-age other kids to do it. "See, George knows that word. George, tell her that word." She would have George tell me.

When questioned about additional strategies that the teacher pro-vided, Susie reported the teacher's attempt at using a structural analy-sis technique focusing on syllabication. In addition, she was encour-aged to use picture clues as a vehicle for informed guessing. She also elaborated on the use of silent reading as a means for improving com-prehension. Each successive failure reinforced her position as an out-cast, as she was constantly humiliated in front of her peers.

Ellen:	Your peers were watching this going on.
Susie:	Mm-hmm.
Ellen:	Did they have any kind of reaction as they watched you struggle through this oral reading situation?
Susie:	I don't remember too much except for impatience sometimes.
Ellen:	And how would they show their impatience?
Susie:	They would say, "Oh, come on." (pause) But I—the—what the teacher did and said hurt more, I think. (pause) I seem to remember more—much more of what the teacher did, Mrs. Koonz—
Ellen:	What would she say?
Susie:	"You're just not trying." "You know that word." And she's always the one—the one that put me on the spot, not the kids.
Ellen:	What does "putting on the spot" mean to you?
Susie:	Well, I mean, we had to take turns in reading group.
Ellen:	She put you on the spot by making you read aloud.
Susie:	Yeah. And then reading silently—oh, when we came to learning to read silently, I was clueless!

You mean you're supposed to look at this and then . . . I was absolutely floored that this kid over here was able to say this was going on and this is—I'm just going, "What? How?" And it was just like a total jaw-dropping thing. I had no clue.

Ellen: So when you were looking at those words, reading silently, what were you thinking?

Susie: Well, I wasn't even—I didn't even know I was supposed to look at the words, I think.

Ellen: What would you do?

Susie: I might kind of look around to see what other kids were doing and try to get clues from that.

Recent research shows that 59% of kindergarten through eighth-grade teachers surveyed admitted to still using round robin reading or a variation of the technique (Ash, Kuhn, & Walpole, 2009). Round robin reading is a teacher-directed, transmission strategy in which the teacher calls on students one after another to read one paragraph, one page, or a section of text from one heading to another. Students who are not reading orally are asked to follow along silently with the reader. Readers who struggle often lose their place, and proficient readers are either bored or read ahead of the group. Susie has vivid memories of how reading instruction was transmitted in her classroom as well as her visceral reaction to ability grouping.

Susie: I was just thinking, you know, it was the whole reading group thing. You know, who's in the best reading group; who's in the—who's struggling.

Ellen: So you were divided out into groups.

Susie: Mm-hmm. A little bit, mm-hmm. But I had better strategies than—I'm just thinking, because Mary Ellen Porter was in my second-grade class, and she had more troubles than I did. And—and I knew she wasn't dumb. But then, you know, I had troubles and I felt dumb, so—who knows.

Ellen: You were in the same reading group with Mary Ellen?

Susie: Sometimes. It kind of—you know, if—if you . . . Yeah, sometimes.

Ellen:	But your best friends were not in your reading group?
Susie:	No.
Ellen:	Were they in the top group?
Susie:	Probably, yeah. Yes. Forget the "probably." Yes, they were.
Ellen:	What else do you remember being in reading group?
Susie:	Figuring out where I was going to be reading.
Ellen:	Was it predictable enough for you to be able to do that?
Susie:	No, I don't think so.
Ellen:	You never knew what you were going to have to read, and so when it came time for you, you had never had a chance to read through it?
Susie:	Except for the pictures.
Ellen:	And you'd already looked through all of those.
Susie:	And I may or may not be following along the words—where the words are, tracking.
Ellen:	So how did you know when it was your turn to read?
Susie:	Well, I hoped—I always hoped I was at the beginning of the page.
Ellen:	So you assumed that they were going to read an entire page?
Susie:	You know when we turn the page. Or you can also look at the—where the kid's finger is.
Ellen:	That helped you.
Susie:	Yes.
Ellen:	Were you ever chastised for not being in the right place?
Susie:	Oh, of course.
Ellen:	How would that happen?
Susie:	"Pay attention, you're—you're not in the right place."
Ellen:	Would she ever skip you because you were on the wrong page?
Susie:	Never, no.
Ellen:	So she would always get you where you needed to be.
Susie:	Mm-hmm. For better or for worse.

Organizing reading instruction through ability grouping escalates the stigma associated with being an undiagnosed dyslexic. Children in low groups typically have fewer opportunities to read while students in higher groups spend more time on critical thinking and read almost double the amount of low-ability groups (Allington & Cunningham, 1996). Susie reveals a myriad of diversionary tactics to avoid the discomfort of reading aloud. When diversion no longer worked, Susie used strategies such as watching when the page was turned or looking to see where another child had placed his finger to determine where her oral reading should begin.

Ellen:	So it's your turn to read. Tell me what's going on within you.
Susie:	Ooooooh. *(nervous/squirmy sound)*
Ellen:	Tell me about that.
Susie:	Wanting to weasel out of it.
Ellen:	And did you ever?
Susie:	I'm sure I did.
Ellen:	Can you remember any weaseling that you might have done to avoid reading orally?
Susie:	Oh, "I need a tissue," you know. "Oh, my—something's wrong with my eye," or "I need to go to the bathroom."
Ellen:	So were you successful in weaseling out?
Susie:	Sometimes.
Ellen:	What about the times you couldn't weasel out.
Susie:	It just hurt my stomach, you know. And sometimes— and sometimes I did a good job. I don't know why. Sometimes things made more sense than others.

Susie's behavioral traits revealed the possibility of comorbid conditions of ADHD and dyslexia. Wilcutt and Pennington (2000) reported that there is a relationship between inattention and reading disabilities in both boys and girls. The irony is that there are fewer referrals for those girls who are most likely to present with dyslexia. The implications for these findings are important when considering the overlap of symptoms of ADHD and dyslexia. The secondary characteristics of dyslexia and ADHD in girls can have a profound impact on their adolescent literacy experience as well as their negotiation of peers, as we'll see as we follow Susie's story further.

Susie Negotiates Peers

The world of school functions as multiple contexts of meaning within which social encounters have significance and people's positions matter. Activities relevant to this world take meaning from it and are situated in particular times and places (Holland et al., 1998). The playground is a significant place for social encounters. Susie modestly reveals her high status outside the classroom and explains how she was quickly repositioned when recess began.

Susie:	I was good on the playground, OK? There were other things I could do.
Ellen:	How were you good on the playground?
Susie:	I was good at playing games. I was good at encouraging people. I was (pause) you know, among the top.
Ellen:	You were a top athlete on the playground?
Susie:	Well, I wouldn't say "athlete," but the encouragers, you know.
Ellen:	You were coaching?
Susie:	Well, and you say, "Oh, yes, you can do it! Come on!"—one of those kind of kids.
Ellen:	You were Queen of the playground.
Susie:	Well, not Queen. I was kind of the—the ladies-in-waiting, kind of.

Susie's privileged position outside the classroom was short lived. The move to junior high intersected with significant family issues. Her father lost his job, and her clothes no longer measured up with those of her peers.

Performing literacy required extensive interpersonal political maneuvering and impression management. McCarthey (2001) demonstrated how students' perceptions of literacy abilities as well as their sense of the perceptions held by their parents and teachers of those same abilities influenced their broader sense of self. High status is often accorded to the position of proficient reader in the Western world. Literacy has often been used to distinguish the elite within a society. These advantages inform the selection of "good reader" as the aspirational position for the undiagnosed dyslexic. To attain this position requires a complex management system rife with diversionary tactics. Susie summarizes this complexity of social positioning in simple terms. "Well, you know, you have this whole thing, and—in school that says, you know, smart is good. Dumb is bad. And reading seems to be that determiner."

Particular ways of acting upon and acting with literacy place individuals and social groups into hierarchical positions within society (Compton-Lilly, 2007). Compton-Lilly (2007) suggested that these positions are indicators of social reading capital. Membership in groups with high levels of social reading capital require the appearance of possessing good reading skills. In addition, social reading capital involves the ability to recognize, access, and utilize social relationships that support the reader. Once established, these social networks provide access to social, economic, and political power that are intrinsic to relationships with family members, teachers, and peers.

The Rest of Susie's Story

Susie went through her entire schooling experience with no formal assistance and without ever reading a book. She now works in a therapeutic learning center, where she's come to recognize her own experiences among the individuals with whom she works.

Ellen:	So you passed all the way through schooling without anyone ever knowing.
Susie:	Well, see—I don't remember anybody ever just talking to me about me. You know, that just—it wasn't part of the picture. I was invisible.
Ellen:	Tell me about being at the therapeutic learning center and somebody finally recognizing that you are dyslexic.
Susie:	Well—when I first started here—I said—I do that—and then I found that—that there's just a whole pattern going on.

Ellen:	That was a supportive experience?
Susie:	Absolutely. Yeah.
Ellen:	Was it freeing? What was your reaction when you all of a sudden had a name to put on your struggles?
Susie:	Well, actually, I think I had the name because of my little brother. He was the diagnosed. Yeah. The designator.
Ellen:	So you knew that you were dealing with this same thing.
Susie:	Yeah. Or at least, a version of it.
Ellen:	When you were diagnosed as well—tell me about that.
Susie:	It was just nice. I felt very clever. I had figured that out by myself, all myself.

Molly

Molly Negotiates Reading

Molly's experience with reading instruction was quite different than that of Susie and Lucy, as Molly experienced the influence of the whole language reading movement. According to Gaffney and Anderson (2000), whole language was at its peak between 1986 and 1996 but began waning in 1996. Even at its most popular, whole language defied definition by those who attempted to study it objectively (Stahl & Miller, 1989). Whole language is primarily a system of beliefs and intentions related to the acquisition of literacy (Goodman, 1993). Goodman (1967) and Smith (1982) asserted that meaning and purpose should be the salient goals in early reading instruction. This view of reading was based on Goodman's (1967) assertion that there are three cueing systems of language that reside in the text. This model proposed that the three cueing systems needed to read were the graphophonic system, the semantic system, and the syntactic system. The graphophonic system provided visual and sound input. The syntactic system provided a linguistic structure and context in sentences. The semantic system transmitted meaning. This cueing system model is embedded in the rationale for whole language approaches to reading instruction.

Goodman (1967) expanded this psycholinguistic model of reading into what he interpreted as a psycholinguistic guessing game. Contrary to phonetic based models, Goodman asserted that efficient reading did not result from precise perception and identification of individual graphic elements, but from skill in selecting the fewest, most productive cues necessary to produce accurate guesses. The anticipation of that which has not been seen was an important component of this model.

This theoretical framework for reading predominated when Molly learned to read. Schools were ready to throw out basal readers, phonics workbooks, spelling programs, and other canned material so that teachers could create individualized reading instruction with authentic children's literature. A literature-based program supported the whole-part-whole constructivist stance contending that the whole of any phenomenon cannot be broken into parts then added together while maintaining the essence of the whole. Under this whole language instruction, Molly explained that she learned to rely on memorization as her only reading strategy:

> I just never understood the words and how to break it down. It was kind of a continuous thing for me, not comprehending. Um, after I was a little bit older, I had a really hard time with chemistry because the words were very strange for me, and I didn't understand it. If it didn't have to do with anything that I could—like history, I could memorize all that. That was very easy for me. But anything else was very hard.

This was the first information gleaned from Molly regarding the specific nature of her negotiation of text. She revealed a word-level struggle and suggested that she saw a relationship between word-level difficulty and passage comprehension. When asked what would have been the kind of instruction that would have helped her be a better reader, her response was simple. She responded, "Just, sounding out, you know, words, letters, going over the nouns."

When asked about oral reading, Molly's comments insinuated abandonment by teachers while facing terror, nerves, and desperation. She reflected some level of understanding for why she was abandoned. She knew they wanted her to do something, but she was unable to meet their expectations. The "shut down" phenomenon was alluded to in this exchange. She predicted future situations like this one. She also formed expectations that teachers were not to be relied upon for help.

Ellen:	How was that when you were asked to read out loud?
Molly:	Terrifying. Well, I mean, I got very nervous, and of course I made it 10 times worse, and you know, all the times I'd look up at the teacher for help and never got any.
Ellen:	What would you want her to do?
Molly:	Something. I never got a response. They wanted me to do it on my own, which I did understand, but help me sound it out or go through that process. I shut down.
Ellen:	What do you mean by that, you "shut down"?
Molly:	Well, I was very embarrassed, and, you know, I thought . . . all through school that's what it was going to be about. In my head I didn't think teachers helped as much as they should've.

Although research has been completed on teacher-student interactions from a variety of perspectives (Cochran-Smith, 1984; Cohen, 1972; Grant & Rothenberg, 1986; O'Connor & Michaels, 1993), more research is needed that connects these interactions with the literate identities of undiagnosed dyslexics. It is daunting to know that the words and actions of a teacher can have such a powerful impact on a student.

Molly Negotiates Family

Molly grew up in a middle class suburban neighborhood in a traditional family replete with the requisite mother, father, and one sister. When questioned about her family's knowledge of her reading difficulties, she took a particularly protective stance. She acknowledged that "my mom definitely knew something was wrong," but excused her mother's lack of action because her teachers characterized her as "a sweet kid." When probed as to how she knew that her mother had knowledge of her difficulties she explained that the signs were obvious:

> Probably just difficulty with homework. Um, I'd have to ask her that. Um, just like grades. She could tell in the reading classes they weren't very good. Um, the math wasn't good, because I felt—I used to kind of read the numbers backwards, so I really have to concentrate, especially when I'm doing the numbers. I'm not sure —at first my dad didn't know. I knew my mom did, and eventually my dad did.

From the earliest of studies, it has been recognized that dyslexia often runs in families (Hallgren, 1950; Hinshelwood, 1917). Reading disabilities were often found in siblings and multiple generations of families. More recent investigations have confirmed the familial basis of dyslexia (Gilger, Pennington, & DeFries, 1991). These studies show that a sibling of a dyslexic child has a 40% chance of having dyslexia and a parent of a dyslexic child has a 30%–40% possibility of having dyslexia (Pennington & Lefly, 2001).

I asked Molly if there was a history of dyslexia in her family. She revealed a probable occurrence, but she was guarded as to full disclosure of those affected. She became quite defensive when questioned regarding the possibility that her mother might be dyslexic.

Ellen:	Do you have any suspicions about other family members?
Molly:	I think my grandfather was.
Ellen:	Why do you think that?
Molly:	Just when we were kids reading books and stuff, he didn't know a lot of words. I don't know if that's dyslexia or the way he was in school, or I don't know.
Ellen:	This is your father's father?

Molly:	Mother's father.
Ellen:	Mother's father. But your mother doesn't have dyslexia?
Molly:	No. Oh no. Our parents read books and they can read a whole page forward and back. My sister can, too, and I'm always amazed by that, because I'm like, wow, how did you do that?
Ellen:	So, your maternal grandfather was dyslexic?
Molly:	I think.
Ellen:	Does your mother have any brothers or sisters?
Molly:	My mother has a sister.
Ellen:	Are there any issues? Does she have children?
Molly:	Yes. And they're straight A's.
Ellen:	No one else?
Molly:	My cousin, I don't think he had a learning disability, but there's something wrong with him.

After Molly was finally diagnosed with dyslexia, she harbored some unresolved resentment toward her parents. Osman (1997) suggested that the presence of a child with dyslexia in the family has a profound influence on family dynamics. This influence extends to the social and emotional development of siblings. There is increased likelihood of adverse familial effects when there are only two children, one of whom has a disabling condition, and when the children are the same sex and close in age. Such was the familial structure in Molly's family. Her sister, younger by one year, is the favored child, at least by her mother. Although lacking—and often envying—the social status of Molly, the sister excelled academically. The focus on the sister's high academic achievement and denial of the underachievement of Molly reflected the need by her parents to maintain an illusion of the family's honor.

Molly:	I was angry with my parents for a while, but I'm not anymore. I was angry at everything once I found out.
Ellen:	You were angry at your parents for not knowing?
Molly:	Well, I think my mom always said that she knew something was wrong, but she would go to the teachers and they would say, "No. She's so sweet.

	Don't worry about it." So, I think I didn't know that for the longest time.
Ellen:	That she had gone to the teachers?
Molly:	Yeah. So—
Ellen:	She didn't talk to you about it?
Molly:	Yeah.
Ellen:	And you didn't talk to her about it?
Molly:	Right.
Ellen:	Why do you think that was the case?
Molly:	I still don't know. It's just my personality. I just hold that stuff in. That's the way I am. I'm just like my father. My mom and my sister love to talk and all this stuff. I just don't want to do it. I mean, I talk, but not. I don't know.
Ellen:	So, did your dad ever intervene?
Molly:	Oh, no.
Ellen:	Would he go to the teachers with her?
Molly:	I'm sure he didn't, because he always worked late.

Molly revealed conflict between her resistance to the stigma assigned to the position of dyslexic and the help disclosure would provide. She harbored resentment toward all of the adults who failed to come to her assistance in her early years. It is possible to blame the victim and interpret the desire to hide her identity as an unskilled reader as her own choice. The need to maintain the facade of proficient reader and to avoid stigma took precedence over the assertive act of asking for help. The performances that she needed to enact in order to hide, maintain, or promote a specific identity among her peers, teachers, or family members were more important than the actual act of reading.

Molly Negotiates Stigma and Shame

The ways students identify themselves as readers, and the ways they want others to identify them, can influence their decisions related to expenditure of effort (Moje & Dillon, 2006). Performance-based classrooms encourage students to enact specific identities in order to be successful, and struggling readers may not believe they can or should take on those identities. Leigh's (2006) study of the ways teachers transacted with students in relation to the reading task revealed that teacher behaviors were influenced by the teacher's perception of the student's cognitive strengths and weaknesses as a reader and how motivated the teacher thought the student was in trying to apply behaviors that might increase comprehension. The teachers described by Molly would express frustration when she did not comply with literacy rituals. She reported that teachers often incorrectly attributed her refusal to comply with their directions as laziness. Molly expressed keen awareness of when effort was put forth and when effort was withheld. When asked about her perception of what working hard meant, she defined the process and motivation with great clarity. Her memories were equally intense as she recalled memories of not working hard.

Molly: I know sixth grade, I remember trying really hard, not that I didn't anyways, but just really trying to understand everything. And I remember history I was always really good at because it was just memorization. I really liked our teacher.

Ellen: How do you define working hard?

Molly: Just putting in an extra couple of hours trying to understand it or asking somebody. I wouldn't do it very often, but I do remember in middle school—I don't know if it was fifth grade or when it was, but just trying.

Ellen: Were there times you didn't work hard?

Molly: I'm sure. Oh yeah. Definitely. I just gave up. People gave up on me, so . . .

There is a research void relative to the metacognitive processes and expenditure of effort of dyslexics during oral and silent reading. There are, however, some insights to be gained from research focused on the generic label of "struggling reader." Hall (2009) admitted that little is known about how struggling readers make decisions about classroom reading tasks. Some researchers related struggling readers' decisions to low motivation, poor self-efficacy, or limited cognitive abilities (Guthrie & Davis, 2003). This framework blamed the victim and suggested that if she developed the appropriate cognitive skills and experienced an increase in motivation and self-efficacy, then she would make more positive decisions about reading and likely improve her abilities.

Organizing reading instruction through ability grouping reinforces this escalating marginalization of the undiagnosed dyslexic. As noted earlier, once a child is assigned to a low group, the chances of moving to a high group are very low (Hiebert, 1983). Molly illustrated the stigma that resulted from ability grouping and how she negotiated the subsequent public shaming. She gave a detailed account of how she negotiated the context of round robin reading.

Molly:	I hated reading aloud.
Ellen:	How did you negotiate the inevitable?
Molly:	I counted the number of students who would read before my turn. I tried to predict which sentences would be mine, and I read and re-read it. I invented other avoidance techniques that I would rely on for years.
Ellen:	Could you describe those techniques?
Molly:	As my turn approached I put my head down.
Ellen:	Was the teacher aware of your anxiety?
Molly:	Probably. She hardly ever called on me.

Like many undiagnosed dyslexic readers, Molly became positioned as a resistant reader. Brozo (2000) explained how resistant readers hide out in secondary school classrooms. Undiagnosed dyslexics, through the marginalizing labels we place upon them, are often set up to become resistant to reading (Alvermann, 2001b). The downward spiral of the undiagnosed dyslexic is exacerbated by teachers making assumptions about students who demonstrate difficulty learning to read. These assumptions may influence the ways in which they interact with these students. As Alvermann (2001b) noted, culture, including school culture, affects one's ability and disability. The consequences of being labeled as disabled in any way are great for a student, and understanding how teacher-student interactions contribute to identity formation is essential to the development of more effective intervention strategies for these students.

Molly Negotiates Peers

Molly was faced with the renegotiation of multiple positions as she entered middle school. Her difficulty with reading and her concomitant academic struggles quickly took a backseat to her social concerns. Molly relished and capitalized on her growing privileged position outside the classroom and was intent on maintaining her position by using connections with other privileged peers (Bourdieu, 1986). Alexander-Passe (2008) reported that dyslexic girls are more affected by social interactions at school, which resulted in higher stress from peer and teacher interactions. The importance of maintaining her privileged social position is evident in this exchange.

Ellen: How were your grades?

Molly: I think they were average, to be honest. I don't know off the top of my head. There might've been a bad grade in one subject, but I think they were—I don't know. Probably C's.

Ellen: Were you concerned about them?

Molly: It wasn't the top thing that was on my mind.

Ellen: What was on your mind?

Molly: Going to middle school. Just meeting boys, cheering, and that kind of stuff. I think fifth grade is when you start to realize that you're—you need to start doing more stuff.

Ellen: It sounds like you were confident in your social position. You didn't have to be anxious about that aspect of your life.

Molly: Yes! That was nice.

The Rest of Molly's Story

Molly ultimately became her high school prom queen and an annual member of the homecoming court. Her bedroom is decorated with artifacts of her gloried high school years. Stacks of yearbooks line her shelves with pages marked that reflect her accomplishments. She is happy "reading her magazines" and has yet to venture into the unknown territory of reading a book. Her literacy experiences have expanded to the creation of a Facebook page and limited use of e-mail.

She has had two unsuccessful attempts at attending college, but the state-mandated reading exam kept her from proceeding past her sophomore year. She now works as a waitress at a restaurant and bar near her home. She shared with her bosses the nature of her dyslexia. With the help of her supervisor, she uses her strong memory skills to memorize the standard menu and any daily changes. Orders are committed to memory as well and repeated verbatim to the cook staff. This is just a brief stop on her planned journey to becoming an interior designer.

Conclusion

Walking in the shoes of undiagnosed dyslexic girls should provide a visceral knowledge of why we can't ignore girls' reading struggles. I hope you have been able to experience firsthand the outcomes of failing to diagnose dyslexia in girls. It has been my goal to provide insights into the true stories of how undiagnosed girls with dyslexia negotiated school with undeveloped literacy skills. The next step is to become aware of how our daughters disguise their reading problems, which we'll discuss in Chapter 3 when we look at how girls aim to "pass" as literate.

Shame and Passing as Literate

Girls with dyslexia will go to unimaginable extremes to avoid the shame of dyslexia. The process of hiding low literacy skills requires extensive interpersonal political maneuvering and impression management. McDermott and Varenne (1995) referred to this process as "passing" as literate. McCarthey (2001) demonstrated how students' perceptions of literacy abilities as well as their sense of the perceptions held by their parents and teachers of those same abilities influenced their broader sense of self. As previously noted, high status is often accorded to the position of proficient reader in the Western world and literacy has often been used to distinguish the elite within a society. Literacy skills place individuals into hierarchical positions within society (Compton-Lilly, 2007). These positions are indicators of relative levels of social reading capital. The elite group is privileged with the ability to recognize, access, and utilize social relationships that support the reader. These social networks provide access to social, economic, and political power. These obvious advantages instill in the dyslexic reader the desire to be perceived as a "good reader." To attain this aspirational position requires a complex management system rife with diversionary tactics. Susie summarized this complexity of social positioning in simple terms: "Well, also, you know, you have this whole thing, and—in school that says, you know, smart is good. Dumb is bad. And reading seems to be that determiner."

Goffman (1959) also contended that most people select fronts that are considered socially acceptable and represent aspects of an ideal identity. Goffman referred to "passing" and "management" activities as the means by which fronts are maintained. Individuals attempting to pass as having a particular identity manage the contexts around them and construct elaborate scenes that provide support to the front identity. One problem for the undiagnosed dyslexic reader is that maintaining the front may take up so much energy that there is little opportunity to make reading one's own.

Themes Related to Passing as Literate

Although some identities are often unconsciously reproduced, others are the result of a conscious practice of figuring the world. This process can be accomplished through the expert use of cultural tools. Once aware of one's position, the individual may choose to remediate and, in doing so, create other ways in which to be positioned. Bakhtin (1981) views this ability to take action as agency. Like Susie, dyslexic pupils are likely to be aware that the position of "good reader" is valued by their culture and peers (Pollard & Filer, 1999) and that diversionary tactics must be used to create and protect their literacy position. To achieve the position of "good reader," Lucy, Susie, and Molly all demonstrated expert use of cultural tools to sustain a presentation of themselves as being more competent readers than they really were and to pass as literate. Three themes emerged related to the ways in which the participants attempted to pass as literate. These included performances that hide, performances that deceive, and performances that leverage learning strengths.

Susie's motivation for passing as literate revolved around the need to be liked and accepted by her peers and significant adults. She admitted to compromising her values and ethics in order to maintain a position of "looking smart" so as not to lose the acceptance and love of the first teacher who had loved her.

Middle school brought more sophisticated ways of passing. With two college-educated parents, Susie came to the classroom with extensive funds of knowledge about the world and how it works. Funds of knowledge are defined by Moll, Amanti, Neff, and Gonzalez (2001) "as the historically accumulated and culturally developed bodies of knowledge and skills essential for household or individual functioning and well-being" (p. 133). In order to "look smart," Susie would make a preemptive strike and ask a "really good question" about some part of the day's lesson about which she had previous knowledge. In doing so, she appeared knowledgeable of and engaged in the assignment. The result was freedom from future questioning regarding unfamiliar text and maintenance of reading capital (Compton-Lilly, 2007). Susie used this technique all the way through college and in doing so avoided the necessity of ever having to read a book.

Institutionalized reading capital (Compton-Lilly, 2007) can be conceptualized as the tangible artifacts that are recognized as evidence of reading proficiency. For Susie, attainment of these artifacts presented a moral and ethical dilemma. Acquiring institutionally sanctioned proficiency benchmarks, such as grades on spelling tests, required the enactment of performances that deceived parents, teachers, and peers. Susie reported that she cheated all the way through third grade and admitted feeling terrible about the act itself. The loss of the admiration of significant others and peers would have proven much more painful.

At its most basic level, passing is a conscious decision to manage identity-related information in a particular context to elicit a specific outcome. Passing also has two other characteristics: (a) it produces a dissonance response because the identity presented through passing conflicts with other identities enacted by the self, and (b) its goal is to project one's conformity with specific characteristics that are dominant or expected in the particular social context (DeJordy, 2008). Molly expressed terror of the potential stigma that would be attached to disclosing the fact that she had difficulty reading. She would rather engage in diversionary tactics and not disclose her secret than to face misunderstanding or underestimation of her potential:

> I think when I was in elementary school I didn't want anyone to think I was different. You know, I didn't want them to think I had a learning problem. Um, I was terrified—I don't know if they still call it Special Ed—because kids were made fun of in Special Ed. You know, as I got older, I probably should've been in Special Ed, but back then I was terrified of that.

Molly was open in her disclosure of cheating as a means to avoid being stigmatized by her peers. She admitted to proficiency in this means of deception. In addition, she reported a sophisticated moral paradigm that provided a sanctioned structure for her deception. Cheating methods varied but those from whom she covertly obtained information needed to adhere to strict qualifications. She also revealed that she possessed the ability to identify her partners in crime.

Molly: I knew how to cheat.

Ellen: How did that happen, that you knew how to cheat? Did someone tell you?

Molly: I think I saw some kids doing it, and I think I just caught on.

Ellen: What were they doing?

Molly: Just looking at someone else's paper. Because our desks were very close together, so it was very easy to kind of put your eyes, you know. I was very good at cheating. Yes. I was very good at that.

Ellen: So, what were some of the ways that you would cheat?

Molly: Well, it sounds cliché, but I would look on someone's paper or go up to a teacher's test and seeing the test right there, just ask very stupid questions to see the paper. We had a French teacher, and that was even harder for me, another language. But she wasn't very—she was an old lady, and she wasn't very, uh, attentive, I guess you could say. And she

> would leave the test right on the desk, and kids
> would just go up and get them—the answers.
>
> *Ellen:* She would leave the answers to the test you were
> about to have?
> *Molly:* Right. Mm-hmm. And she never noticed that all the
> students would go get the answers and put them
> right next to their paper.
> *Ellen:* So, you weren't the only one doing this?
> *Molly:* Well, you could—I could just know when someone
> was cheating or if they were trying, being very
> quiet in the class, not being very focused, I guess
> you could say.
> *Ellen:* That's interesting. So, you felt—you felt as though
> you weren't alone, but there was never any
> communication?
> *Molly:* Right. Yes. Never. There's a—most people don't
> want anyone to know their plots. Or at least that's
> how I saw it. So. I mean, I never got caught . . . um,
> you know, it made me feel even worse just 'cause I
> didn't want to do that . . .
> *Ellen:* But, why did you continue to do it when it made
> you feel worse?
> *Molly:* Because I didn't want a bad grade, because teach-
> ers would know, Mom and Dad would know,
> friends would know, that just seemed a lot worse to
> me in my head.

Molly set specific ethical boundaries on dealing with a culturally unacceptable behavior. She drew the line when cheating involved putting her friends at risk. She also reveals a belief that the smart kids who were outside her peer group deserved her wandering eyes.

> *Ellen:* Do you remember the first time you cheated?
> *Molly:* No. Maybe fourth or fifth grade.
> *Ellen:* So, it was the act of looking at someone else's
> paper and actually taking their answer?
> *Molly:* Right.
> *Ellen:* What was your reaction to that?
> *Molly:* At first I felt really awful. I never would cheat off my
> friend's paper. It was always a very smart person
> who would sit next to me or something.

Ellen:	But you said your friends are very smart, though.
Molly:	Right.
Ellen:	But you wouldn't cheat off of them?
Molly:	No.
Ellen:	Why is that?
Molly:	I don't know. I think it would've made me feel a little worse. I think the smart kids didn't deserve better from—you know.
Ellen:	So, explain to me the difference in what you're talking about as the smart kids and the kids—your friends that were also smart.
Molly:	Well, they were my friends. That's the difference.
Ellen:	OK.
Molly:	The thing was that they were just my friends.
Ellen:	Were the other smart kids running in a different peer group?
Molly:	They were probably outside of my circle.
Ellen:	It sounds like you were into traditional popular kinds of things. You were a cheerleader, went to parties, and then many of your friends were smart on top of that. You had the total package in your friendship group.
Molly:	Right.
Ellen:	OK. And then you've got another group of people who are smart but maybe aren't as socially gifted.
Molly:	Right. I think that's everywhere.
Ellen:	Oh yes. Absolutely. It is everywhere.
Molly:	Yeah but I was also—I don't know. How old are you in sixth grade?
Ellen:	11, 12.
Molly:	Yeah. I was also that age. I still wanted to be with my friends. That was the most important thing.
Ellen:	And you made it through high school?
Molly:	With a 3.0.

Limitations to cheating were also drawn when it came time for Molly to take standardized tests such as the Iowa Tests of Basic Skills (ITBS) and the SAT. The mandate for administering the ITBS was underenforced and as such allowed the use of diversionary tactics (Molly used the excuse of being "sick" to miss the test, for example).

The decision to forgo cheating on the SAT was explained as a desire to measure her true ability. She seemed to have an underlying fear of being caught for the first time in a high-risk setting. The fact that she discovered that all students received different versions of the test also figured into her decision. When she falsified her scores to her peers, she also imposed the ethical barrier of not excessively inflating her actual score.

Ellen: What about your SATs?

Molly: I promised myself that I was not going to cheat, because I figured if I did cheat that day I was going to get caught.

Ellen: But you thought about cheating?

Molly: Yes. But then I found out every test is different. I do not off the top of my head remember my score. It was close—a little below average, I think.

Ellen: But you did it yourself?

Molly: Yes.

Ellen: Completely?

Molly: Mm-hmm.

Ellen: How was that experience?

Molly: I really didn't want to open it when it came in the mail, I didn't want to know. I really didn't. You know, all my friends were, "Oh, I got 1200," or whatever it was. I knew mine wasn't going to be up there.

Ellen: Did you tell them?

Molly: Yes. Just a little bit higher than what it was. To be in the ballpark. I mean, I didn't go overboard. I never went overboard. Never.

Ellen: Why did you make the decision not to cheat on your SATs?

Molly: I think maybe to see how good I was. Um, kind of in the back of my head, I had been cheating for so long. I was like, I'm going to get caught one day and kicked out from school or something like that, and I didn't want that to happen.

Molly further explained her diversionary strategies as she discussed participation in literacy practices with her closest friends. These processes of written and oral production and interpretation of texts provide students with opportunities to create relationships with other classmates (Sperling, 1995) and negotiate their sense of themselves as gendered, raced, and classed beings (Dyson, 1995; Finders, 1997). Through these identity negotiations, they articulate their life goals and interests (Hull & Schultz, 2001), as well as stake out allegiances within larger social groups or discourse communities (Gee, 1996). Molly had limited access to these literacy processes. When asked about peer group participation in reading and writing in diaries, her memories are vivid:

> No. I stayed away from anything I could with that. They all wrote in diaries. I never did. We just talked about boys and watched movies. I never, um, tried to do anything that would show that I couldn't do it. I always wanted to do that, um, but it was just too much. I just knew that there was something wrong with me. I just didn't know what or how to deal with it.

One of the best places to observe adolescence is on the pages of middle school and high school yearbooks. Molly and I spent several afternoons looking through her yearbooks and discussing past and present peer relationships. One afternoon I explained that we were going to focus on fifth, sixth, and seventh grades, and that I was going to ask her to go back, and see if the pictures might activate memories. We started with the faces, many of which had been highlighted. Katie's face and name kept appearing, so I focused on school-related activities with Katie.

Molly:	I met my best friend [Katie] first day of fourth grade, and I remember cheating off of, um, the girl next to her. So, I kept thinking, I hope Katie can't see me. It's a shame that most kids just want to fit in, and there's not much pressure to do good in school anymore.
Ellen:	What is the biggest pressure?
Molly:	Fitting in.

Ellen:	Would you and Katie study together?
Molly:	Yeah. We'd all study together, but there was more a group discussion type of thing, and that was something I could do better.

The study group would typically take place at one friend's house. The girls would all study together in the friend's living room with all of the requisite books and study materials assembled on the coffee table. At this point, the group would discuss the homework or the current book, an activity that was a lifeline for Molly. She "could understand better what was going on." She also acknowledged the purposefulness of this nightly ritual. "I didn't know at the time, but I guess I used them." I tried to assuage her obvious guilt by pointing out that many girls study together, and each girl gained information from the others. The idea of using her friends as a tool to help her gain information seemed to broach the unwritten code of adolescent friendship.

Our conversation turned to another friend, Jennifer. Of the two, Jennifer had an easier time in school. She was also a star athlete. I asked Molly if there was any jealously in the relationship.

Molly:	No. I just didn't understand why I wasn't like that.
Ellen:	What would "like that" be? Tell me what that is.
Molly:	Where I just looked at it a couple of times or—and then got it, and that was it.
Ellen:	And you never mentioned it to anyone?
Molly:	No.
Ellen:	So, you're studying with these two girls who are having a very easy time in school and making straight A's. But you are the "man magnet" as it says in your yearbook. I would imagine they envied you.
Molly:	Mm-hmm. That was—you know, I grew up being jealous of all these smart people. It's nice to have something—
Ellen:	Here you are, you continue to be beautiful and smart, you keep talking about these smart people. It's not smart, though, is it, that was the issue? There's a big difference between being smart and intelligent and having a reading disability, being

> dyslexic. Because you know in certain situations
> you could acquire information.
>
> Molly: I was good in history. I mean, I personally feel his-
> tory is all memorization, and if I could listen to the
> lecture and understand it, would just memorize
> that. I wouldn't read the book, but the lecture was
> going on. I understood it.

The reactions of the undiagnosed dyslexic are often contingent upon the context of the classroom and pedagogical choices of the teacher. Both can influence how the undiagnosed dyslexic reader experiences literacy events. The teacher's interaction with students through his or her lesson structure, questioning patterns, and general talk with students can influence student participation in literacy events (Cazden, 1986). This interaction can occur as a process of transmission or as a process of transaction. The lecture format described by Molly is a transmissional stance. It is often referred to as banking pedagogy (Freire, 1970). From this stance, the instructor assumes the position of the depositor of information and learners are viewed as empty vessels ready to be filled by the information imparted to them. Transmission implies that learning is transmitted from the teacher to the student. The teacher first delivers information and later determines the success of the transmission by employing formalized measures of assessment. For Molly, this transmission of knowledge was her first access to the body of text and provided a pool of knowledge for future discourse in her homework group.

The homework group promoted a different opportunity in that learning was dialogical. Molly could assume the dual roles of learner and teacher. Molly constructed and coconstructed knowledge through these social interactions. This process would be impossible for Molly without the primary transmission of knowledge from the instructor.

Shared Findings on Passing as Literate

The following findings were observed relative to Lucy, Molly, and Susie:

1. Each girl's reading problems were influenced by the reading program currently in vogue, the learning style of the participants, and the teaching style of the teacher.
2. Discussions and oral presentations provided the necessary support to help each girl access and make meaning of text.
3. Expenditure of effort while engaging in literacy tasks varied according to each girl's assessed value of the task and her feelings regarding the person requesting the task.
4. Appearing to be literate was more important than actually being literate.
5. Incidents of literacy shaming were experienced by all of the girls, but how each girl reacted to literacy shaming varied.
6. Strategies used by the girls to "pass as literate" included (a) hiding, (b) deceiving, and (c) using learning strengths.
7. Differences between academic abilities and academic performance resulted in conflicting identities.

School is a social context that provides the social dynamics of the world within which students learn and construct their learner identities (Lave & Wenger, 1998). Lucy's, Molly's, and Susie's worlds of school were "socially and culturally constructed realm[s] of interpretation in which particular characters and actors were recognized, significance assigned to certain acts, and particular outcomes valued over others" (Holland et al., 1998, p. 52). They disclosed the positions that were culturally imposed as well as those that were chosen. Some of these positions required conventional or stereotypical performances. The participants told of instances in which they were denied entry into some worlds based on their social rank or position influenced by their dyslexia. They also told of times when they denied entry to a world to which they belonged to those they deemed unqualified or unworthy outsiders. They told of culture-specific storylines that were exemplified by roles such as student, daughter, sister, or athlete. They revealed their views of the world from the vantage point of each position, at that moment, and in terms of the images, metaphors, stories, and concepts that were relevant to their current situations.

Identity labels can be used to stereotype, privilege, or marginalize readers and writers as "struggling "or "proficient," as "creative" or "deviant" (Lin, 2008). The institution in which one learns to read relies heavily on identities that take the form of progress indicators. These identity labels can be especially powerful in an individual's life. Words, texts, and the literate practices that accompany these labels not only reflect but may also produce the self (Davies, 2003).

Lucy, Molly, and Susie demonstrated reactions to the stress created as a result of the demands of the classroom. All reported incidents of literacy shaming related to oral reading. They told stories of elaborate strategies that they used to avoid the stigma associated with reading orally to maintain their social capital. Relegation to the lowest reading group was a devastating experience for all of the girls. The girls' experiences with ability grouping only added to their growing cognitive dissonance.

Social capital is inherent in the structure of the participants' relations between and among actors in and out of school. Lucy was quick to explain the benefits that her natural leadership abilities, interpersonal skills, and linguistic facility provided. Her social abilities expanded her social capital (Bourdieu, 1986; Coleman, 1988; Field, 2003) enough to warrant her recruitment and repositioning (Holland et al., 1998) into the center of the school's social context despite her reading difficulties.

Susie reached the pinnacle of her social capital as she reigned as a "lady-in-waiting" in the realm of the playground. However, Susie's privileged position outside the classroom was short lived. The move to junior high intersected with significant family issues. It was at this point that Susie learned the passing strategies that would serve her all the way though her college years.

As Molly prepared to go to middle school, her concerns over her difficulty with reading and the concomitant academic struggles were diminished by her new, privileged social status. Molly relished her privileged position outside the classroom and was intent on maintaining her position by using connections with other privileged peers

(Bourdieu, 1986). This concurs with Alexander-Passe's (2008) assertion that dyslexic girls are more affected by social interactions at school than their nondyslexic peers.

According to Morgan and Klein (2001), responses from the peer group can be a powerful influence on the individual's perception of self. The participants confirmed the effect that their peers had on their lives. Dyslexics are seldom allowed to forget they are different. This awareness is reflected in the need for undiagnosed dyslexics to make comparisons with peers and to recognize intuitively their undefined and unacknowledged learning differences. Loneliness and isolation are typical of many undiagnosed dyslexics (Tur-Kaspa, Weisel, & Segev, 1998). This loneliness and isolation often create the need to pass as literate.

Conclusion

Now that you know that your daughter is faced with the dilemma of dealing with her dyslexia in a way that is accepted by her peers, it becomes your job to provide the support that she needs. Opportunities to shine in other aspects of her life will provide moments of authentic social acceptance. Don't allow your daughter to spend so much time maintaining the front of literacy expert that there is little opportunity or energy left for her to actually learn to read. Chapter 4 looks at what can happen when dyslexia and identity struggles, like the need to pass as a reader, collide.

Taking Action Before Dyslexia and Identity Collide

The identities of girls as readers are decided for them (Alvermann, 2001a). Girls are all faced with the dilemma of figuring out into which worlds they will enter temporarily or peripherally and those they will enter with positions of power and prestige. For some, positions are predetermined culturally and socially. This is especially true in the schools of the United States. Undiagnosed dyslexic girls, through the marginalizing labels we place upon them like "struggling" and "reluctant," are often set up to become resistant to reading. As Alvermann (2001b) so aptly stated, "Culture constructs disability, as well as ability" (p. 677).

Our daughters are never taught to consider that their reading troubles might be due to a normal difference in their genes and brains, just like being tall or short. They would never venture to guess that the alphabetic code presents a completely unnatural processing challenge to their brains. Instead they blame themselves. They feel ashamed of themselves and ashamed of their minds. Statements like "I'm dumb," "I'm stupid," "I'm not smart," or "I'm not good in school" are all strategies to protect themselves from the shame they feel. Shame motivates girls to avoid reading. It also fosters self-doubt and undermines the cognitive capacities needed to engage in other academic endeavors. Millions of girls are caught in a downward spiral. Not only are they in danger of being poor readers, they are also in danger of developing aversions to the concept of learning. Shame is disabling, and it can have lifelong debilitating effects.

Molly, Susie, and Lucy looked deeply into their past and gave us uninhibited glances into the world of the undiagnosed dyslexic. As they told their courageous stories of resistance, all three girls revealed how they came to "figure out" their identities. We watched their identities develop within and through social practices in multiple contexts (Boaler & Greeno, 2000; Holland et al., 1998). These girls did not operate in isolation. As members of learning communities, they belonged to more than one world, with boundaries that blurred and overlapped. The paths that these girls traveled zigzagged from victim to queen. For each mile traveled, there were humbling missteps and joyous sprints.

This examination of undiagnosed dyslexics illuminates the ways in which the context of the classroom, teachers, and peers impact literacy identities. This presents a view of literacy identity as an ongoing construction of the self, mediated by contexts in which each girl is engaged. Such a view suggests a more complete picture of what it means to position oneself as a reader. Furthermore, becoming a reader is more than learning a set of skills to be performed on a standardized test. Rather, transforming one's literacy identity "changes who we are by changing our ability to participate, to belong, to negotiate meaning" (Wenger, 1999, p. 226).

Instructional Implications

On the first day of school, a dyslexic child faces a myriad of challenges. She must process oral instructions from teachers and remember them long enough to act on them and finish required tasks. The difficulty of every task is exacerbated by a poor working memory and subsequent unreliable short-term memory. Girls with dyslexia start school at an immediate disadvantage long before the task of reading is introduced (Thomson & Hartley, 1980). The dyslexic girl takes much longer to process information, particularly in reading, where she has to connect letter patterns with associated words. Slow and poor phonological awareness may cause slow and inaccurate processing of the spoken language, slowness to read, and the possibility that she will become so confused that she will resort to copying from others nearby. Problems with fine motor skills may make the dyslexic student look clumsy and, as such, she is open to ridicule from both ill-informed teachers and her peers. The inability to organize and demonstrate on-task behaviors leaves your dyslexic daughter in a vulnerable position with little social capital (Alexander-Passe, 2004).

Long before entering school, most children possess well-developed linguistic competence. They have acquired sophistication in phonology, grammar, word meaning, and pragmatics. Learning to read and write requires attention to the linguistic building blocks of words. Phonemes, the smallest sound units, have no meaning as separate units but when represented by their graphic counterpart, graphemes, written words emerge. Syllables are composed of onsets, which are initial consonants or consonant clusters, followed by rimes, or the vowel and what follows it. In order to read, one must perceive these sound units of spoken language and link them to the corresponding spelling patterns in words. The connections are formed out of the readers' general knowledge of phoneme-grapheme correspondences that recur in many words (Ehri & McCormick, 2004). Given the importance of these linguistic units, educators must determine the linguistic focus and the corresponding instructional activities that offer the highest probability that word recognition will occur.

There is no consensus as to the nature of the optimum beginning reading instruction. Reductionist theorists take a philosophic stance that holds that meanings in the world can be broken down into logical, verifiable sequences, where smaller parts of a phenomenon, when added together, describe and explain the whole phenomenon or meaning (Poplin, 1995). Literacy scholars who embrace the reductionist stance insist that systematic instruction in phonological awareness and phonics benefits the reading accuracy of most children, and it can be taught in various ways (Torgesen et al., 1999). Reductionists assert that systematic phonics instruction helps level the playing field by improving the reading of at-risk children and poor readers (Lyon, 1999).

However, holistic literacy researchers are dubious of the evidence that supports explicit phonics instruction for all children (Poplin, 1995). Their whole-part-whole constructivist stance contends that the whole of any phenomenon cannot be broken into parts then added together while maintaining the essence of the whole. This sequence aligns language development theory to mathematics learning, and forms the basis of the writing process, whole language techniques, inquiry-based science, and authentic assessment movements in education (Smith, 1982).

As the dyslexic girl matures, new and equally challenging decisions face literacy educators. For those who begin the intermediate grades with weak word recognition skills or poor fluency, the challenges of intermediate-level reading can lead to or exacerbate reading difficulties and lower achievement in reading (Snow, Burns, & Griffin, 1998). The demand to read more complex texts increases in the fourth and fifth grades (Allington, 2001). Likewise, teachers at these grade levels require students to do more independent reading and independent learning from their reading as the shift from "learning to read" to "reading to learn" takes hold (NICHD, 2000). Students with lower achievement in reading in the intermediate grades continue to experience reading difficulties throughout high school and adulthood. Snow, Burns, and Griffin (1998) suggested that students with reading difficulties are more likely than those without reading difficulties to drop out of school. They presented a compelling argument that dropping out of school is not a one-time, one-moment phenomenon, but a situation that begins early in one's school career when the efforts to attain a kind of school literacy that reflects high-level thinking about texts go awry. Stanovich (1986) clarified this phenomenon by explaining that reading difficulties overshadow reading strengths when word recognition strategies compete with memory capacity for higher level functions such as comprehension. This results in a painstaking effort by the reader to merely "get through" the text. Slow, capacity-draining word-recognition processes monopolize the reader's cognitive resources, leaving little to focus on higher level processes of text integration and comprehension.

If the alphabetic principle, which facilitates rapid word recognition, is slow to be acquired and internalized or is not practiced sufficiently, students extend more of their cognitive energies to making sense of the words instead of the text. This phenomenon is also known as word-level comprehension failure (Pressley, 2002). Pressley (2002) emphasized that students in the intermediate grades who still struggle with word recognition read less because reading becomes unrewarding, thus practice with reading is avoided, precluding eventual growth and development. Stanovich (2000) described this phenomenon as a "downward spiral" for students, suggesting that if word-level difficulties are not overcome, then the students' experiences with reading become worse.

What we know about stopping this downward spiral is limited. The National Reading Panel (2000) emphasized the importance of keeping adolescents' interests and needs in mind when designing effective literacy instruction at the middle and high school levels. The following insights add to the growing complexity of providing appropriate literacy instruction in the 21st century (Alvermann, 2001a):

➤ Adolescents' perceptions of how competent they are as readers and writers, generally speaking, will affect how motivated they are to learn in their subject area classes (e.g., the sciences, social studies, mathematics, and literature). Thus, if academic literacy instruction is to be effective, it must address issues of self-efficacy and engagement.

➤ Adolescents respond to the literacy demands of their subject area classes when they have appropriate background knowledge and strategies for reading a variety of texts. Effective instruction develops students' abilities to comprehend, discuss, study, and write about multiple forms of text (print, visual, and oral) by taking into account what they are capable of doing as everyday users of language and literacy.

➤ Adolescents who struggle to read in subject area classrooms deserve instruction that is developmentally, culturally, and linguistically responsive to their needs. To be effective, such instruction must be embedded in the regular curriculum and address differences in their abilities to read, write, and communicate orally as strengths, not as deficits.

➤ Adolescents' interests in the Internet, hypermedia, and various interactive communication technologies (e.g., chat rooms where people can take on various identities unbeknown to others) suggest the need to teach youth to read with a critical eye toward how writers, illustrators, and the like represent people and their ideas—in short, how individuals who create texts make those texts work. At the same time, it suggests teaching adolescents that all texts, including their textbooks, routinely promote or silence particular views.

➤ Adolescents' evolving expertise in navigating routine school literacy tasks suggests the need to involve them in higher level thinking about what they read and write than is currently possible within a transmission model of teaching, with its emphasis on skill and drill, teacher-centered instruction, and passive learning. Effective alternatives to this model include participatory approaches that actively engage students in their own learning (individually and in small groups) and that treat texts as tools for learning rather than as repositories of information to be memorized (and then all too quickly forgotten). (p. 2)

Power of Discourse

The assertion that effective instruction develops students' abilities to comprehend, discuss, study, and write about multiple forms of text (print, visual, and oral) by taking into account what they are capable of doing as everyday users of language and literacy is supported by the experiences of Lucy, Molly, and Susie. They provided multiple examples of how the context of the classroom and the pedagogical choices made by the teacher are critical in influencing how the struggling reader experiences a literacy event. Aspects of the teacher and the activity determined whether these girls considered an event worthy of effort. This decision in turn determined their level of participation in the literacy event and ultimately their literate identities. The affinity of these girls for engagement in peer discussions reinforces the efficacy of discussion as an instructional approach for dyslexic readers. Discussion provides contexts where dyslexic readers may acquire a more complete understanding of the text, practice comprehension strategies in organic ways, and engage in high-level thinking about text.

Applebee and colleagues (2003) examined the relationships between student literacy performance and discussion-based approaches to the development of understanding in 64 middle and high school English classrooms. A series of hierarchical linear models indicated that discussion-based approaches were significantly related to spring semester performance, controlling for fall semester performance and other background variables. These approaches were effective across a range of situations and for low-achieving as well as high-achieving students, although interpretations were complicated because instruction is unequally distributed across tracks. Overall, the results suggested that students whose classroom literacy experiences emphasized discussion-based approaches in the context of high academic demands internalize the knowledge and skills necessary to engage in challenging literacy tasks on their own.

Lucy, Molly, and Susie reinforce the way authentic conversation provides a means for the dyslexic reader to engage in high-level thinking to the same extent as their peers. The classrooms in which the dyslexic reader, her peers, and her teachers created contexts that supported discussions provided the opportunity for all to be invested participants in classroom literacy acts. Researchers have begun to conceptualize literacy instruction of dyslexics from a Vygotskian (1978) perspective. This view places emphasis on constructing meaningful activities in a social community that uses dialogic interaction to scaffold learning (Englert & Palincsar, 1991; Poplin, 1995; Stone & Harris, 1991). Although these principles have been studied in a range of interactive literacy contexts (Au & Kawakami, 1985; Palincsar & Brown, 1984), few researchers have extended them to the instruction of students who are nonreaders and nonwriters.

Dyslexic readers thrive as thinkers about text in discussions that include engagement in problem solving. Through this engagement, they are able to approach their Zone of Proximal Development (ZPD). The ZPD defines those functions that have not yet matured but are in the process of maturation; functions that will mature tomorrow but are currently in an embryonic state. These functions could be termed the "buds" or "flowers" of development rather than the "fruits" of development (Vygotsky, 1978, p. 86). The ZPD is an open space of responsiveness such as peers meeting over a shared literacy task, providing communicative challenges to each other, or simply exploring new texts. By being positioned in her ZPD, the dyslexic reader can move from the position of powerlessness to solve problems on her own to a position of power from which she can solve problems, albeit with assistance. Similarly, to make learning available, instructors must bring new material and skills into a zone of intelligibility, possible participation, and motivated interaction.

Teachers need to understand ways to encourage discourse that elicits genuine problem solving about the meanings of text. Teachers need to understand the discourse features that indicate high-level thinking to model and discuss the features in their work with dyslexic students during discussions about literary texts. Discourse provides the necessary intellectual scaffolds for dyslexic readers who use talk as a tool to make meaning. The talk during the discussions provides opportunities for participants in the discussions to draw on their knowledge of reading comprehension strategies and to use those strategies in authentic or organic ways during the discussions. The contextual foundations of the discussions provided opportunities for the dyslexic readers to think in high-level ways.

Vygotsky's (1978) work suggested that cognitive functions appear first on a social plane—between people—before going underground as they are internalized. Within this process, language and discourse become the primary tools by which teachers mediate performance. These same tools are then used by students to mediate their own performance. Talk that was once socially enacted between teachers and students is subsequently enacted by the student in private. Molly and her study group gave an excellent example of this process. Through these processes, the words and regulatory functions originally performed by the teacher become internalized by the students as they assert their voices in the learning community.

Thus, classroom dialogue helps to achieve a context in which the dyslexic student can experience full participation. To further ensure this participation, the nature of instruction should provide an opportunity for the involvement of dyslexic girls in holistic and contextualized activities, participation in school-based discourse, the interaction of teachers and students through scaffolded dialogues, and a social context that promotes full membership in the literacy community. In this pursuit, discourse provides the necessary mechanism to light the way for the dyslexic reader.

Obviously, teaching reading to dyslexic readers is a job for an expert. Learning to read is a complex linguistic achievement. Moreover, teaching reading requires considerable knowledge and skill, acquired over several years through focused study and supervised practice. No one can develop such expertise by taking one or two college courses, or attending a few one-time in-service workshops. Although reading is the cornerstone of academic success, a single course in reading methods is often all that is offered most prospective teachers. Even if well taught, a single course is only the beginning. The demands of competent reading instruction, and the training experiences necessary to learn it, have been seriously underestimated by universities and by those who have approved licensing programs. The consequences for teachers and students alike have been disastrous. We will discuss this more in Chapter 5.

Sharon and Strategies to Support Girls Who Struggle

I would like to share a final story of a woman we will call Sharon. Sharon is a longtime friend and learned of my book in its final stages. In addition to her myriad community service activities, Sharon has raised a large family; some of the children suffer with varying degrees of dyslexia. She explains that dyslexia made her who she is while simultaneously motivating her to seek out help for her children.

> I'm tough—people don't hurt me when they say negative things or whatever. It really has made me who I am. My saving grace was outside of the classroom I was well-liked, had tons of friends. I could play sports, you know I was well accepted. I felt like everybody liked me. I was Momma's right-hand man growing up. I had nine brothers and sisters. I don't know what she'd have done without me. I took care of those kids in the backyard, 24/7, when she needed it, and loved every minute of it. I felt so important. I was her go to person to help. I made plays up. I was the director and I'd make all the kids do things, I'd take them on fieldtrips. We'd go down to the park and all the neighborhood would come with us. Can you imagine that today?

Sharon exemplifies the strategies parents can use to support their dyslexic daughters. These include the strategies of (a) obtaining a definitive diagnosis and relating that diagnosis to the child, (b) acknowledging the power of shame, (c) encouraging their child's natural abilities and talents, and (d) advocating for their children at school.

Obtaining a Definitive Diagnosis

> The common theme any time you talk to an adult that was undiagnosed with any kind of learning disability was they didn't know what was wrong with them. They didn't understand, their parents didn't understand. And because of that, not knowing what's wrong and why you couldn't learn, there was fear and self-doubt in the classroom.—Sharon

Many parents of dyslexic girls are unaware that their daughter may have a recognizable pattern of difficulties that can be significantly alleviated through the learning of appropriate skills and strategies. Typically, the parent feels thoroughly confused. You know your daughter is bright and quick-thinking but apparently quite slow in reading.

If you suspect that your child has dyslexia, you will want to seek testing and a diagnosis. Because the symptoms and degree of severity of dyslexia are variable, there is no one test or approach that will provide a definitive diagnosis. Rather, there are a variety of different approaches to measuring, defining, and understanding the learning profile and needs of each child. As a parent, you will find that a highly individualized approach is needed, depending on your child's specific symptoms and learning problems. You may need a multidisciplinary approach, such as having your child evaluated by several different kinds of learning and medical specialists. There is no one test that can diagnose dyslexia. You will need to consider a number of diagnostic sources. These will vary according to the educational, psychological, or medical professional that you contact. These sources might include:

- ➤ *Answers to a number of questions.* These will likely include questions about your child's development, education, and medical history. The doctor may also want to know about any conditions that run in your child's family and may ask if any family members have a learning disability.
- ➤ *Questionnaires.* Your child's doctor may have your child, family members, or teachers answer written questions. Your child

may be asked to take tests to identify his or her reading and language abilities.

➤ *Vision, hearing, and neurological (brain) tests.* These can help determine whether another disorder may be causing or adding to your child's poor reading ability.

➤ *Psychological testing.* The professional may ask you or your child questions to better understand your child's psychological state. This can help determine whether social problems, anxiety, or depression may be limiting your child's abilities.

➤ *Testing for reading and other academic skills.* Your child may take a set of educational tests and have the process and quality of his or her reading skills analyzed by a reading expert.

A good place to start is your pediatrician. She can provide trusted resources for you to contact to obtain a comprehensive diagnosis. Take some time to prepare for your first visit. As you prepare, the Mayo Clinic (2012) suggested the following might prove helpful:

➤ Write down any symptoms that your child is experiencing, including any that may seem unrelated to the reason for which you scheduled the appointment.

➤ Write down key personal information, including any major stresses or recent life changes.

➤ Make a list of any medications, as well as any vitamins or supplements that your child is taking.

➤ Ask a family member or friend along, if possible. Sometimes it can be difficult to soak up all of the information provided to you during an appointment. Someone who accompanies you may remember something that you missed or forgot.

➤ Write down questions to ask your doctor.

Preparing a list of questions ahead of time can help you make the most of your appointment. For dyslexia, some basic questions to ask your doctor include:

➤ Why is my child having difficulty reading and understanding?

➤ What kinds of tests does he or she need?

➤ Can dyslexia be treated?

> ➢ Are there any alternatives to the primary approach that you're suggesting?
> ➢ How quickly will we see progress?
> ➢ Are there any brochures or other printed material that I can take home with me? Can you recommend any websites?
> ➢ Will my other children have dyslexia, too?
> ➢ What kind of help can I expect from my child's school for dyslexia?

Your doctor will likely have a number of questions for you as well, such as:

> ➢ When did you first notice that your child was having trouble reading? Did a teacher bring it to your attention?
> ➢ At what age did your child start talking?
> ➢ Have you noticed if your child writes any letters or words in reverse?
> ➢ Have you tried any reading interventions? If so, which ones?
> ➢ Have you noticed any behavior problems or social difficulties you suspect may be linked to your child's trouble reading?
> ➢ Has your child had any vision problems?

Sharon sought help for her eldest son. She explained that he has the worst case of dyslexia in the family. He was turned down from the one school that could help him. Testing seemed the only recourse.

> Finally I had him tested by a friend of mine. I was telling her about all the problems. She said bring him to me and let me test him, so we did, and we went in and they said he is severely dyslexic. He is doing this, this, this, and this, and I went "Oh my god, that's what I do." And they said, "How long have you been doing that?" I said, "My whole life," and they said, "Well, this is where he gets it from." So for the first time, when he was diagnosed—it had a name. And I knew that there was a reason for my problem. The

burden was lifted. The greatest thing was that with this knowledge I was able to help him.

There are several different tests that may be used to evaluate your child. They are not necessarily specific to dyslexia, but when combined, they help provide a good picture of your child's development. An evaluator will often start with an IQ test to determine your child's overall ability level. One of the most commonly used tests is the Wechsler Intelligence Scale for Children (WISC-IV). It breaks down scores into two scales, Verbal and Performance, which in turn each consist of various subtests. This testing will also provide a full-scale IQ score.

The Verbal Scale measures language expression, comprehension, listening, and the ability to apply these skills to solving problems. The Performance Scale assesses nonverbal problem solving, perceptual organization, speed, and visual-motor proficiency. It includes tasks like puzzles, picture analysis, imitating designs with blocks, and copying. This test is given orally, by an evaluator working individually with your child, so your child does not have to know how to read to score well on the test.

By looking at the scores on various subtests, the evaluator will see a pattern of strengths and weaknesses. This sort of testing is extremely valuable for all children and can be used to indicate a wide variety of learning disabilities. Dyslexia is indicated as a possible diagnosis if the subtests show that a child has particular weakness in areas normally associated with dyslexia such as verbal fluency, short-term auditory memory (digit span), or speed of processing information.

Your child will also be given achievement tests to measure reading performance. The specific tests will vary depending on the preferences of the evaluator and the age of your child. Younger children will be given tests that measure prereading and early reading skills, such as simple word recognition tests. Older children may be given tests that measure sentence reading, oral fluency, and reading comprehension.

There are also some specialized tests geared toward measuring problems commonly associated with dyslexia. Included will be tests of phonemic awareness. Your child may be asked to read nonsense words that represent major decoding patterns. The use of nonsense words eliminates the chance of an invalid diagnosis. Nonsense words preclude the chance of confusing memorized sight vocabulary with true decoding skills. A complete assessment will include tests that assess word retrieval skills and auditory and verbal processing speed. Tests of rapid automatic naming are clinically significant and provide clout to a definitive diagnosis of dyslexia. Short-term memory, or digit span, might also be tested. These tests ask children to remember and repeat a short sequence of letters or numbers or to identify a sequence of letters, numbers, or pictures after briefly viewing a picture or card with the sequence. The results of these tests should be explained in detail in a formal report. Included will be a diagnosis of dyslexia if appropriate and a listing of suggested interventions.

Acknowledging the Power of Shame

Sharon experienced shame firsthand. She went into detail describing her avoidance of situations that might result in a shaming experience. She credited her strong personality and resiliency as her salvation in the face of shame.

> My saving grace was, I have a very strong personality. I was well-liked. Um, other than the classroom, I was a happy camper. It is harder for those who don't have strong personalities, who go inward, and feel bad about themselves. I only felt bad about myself in the classroom. And I was funny, I had a great sense of humor, and I drove the teachers crazy with that sense of humor. I would make jokes and laugh at myself, and laugh at others. Find humorous things in everything, in order not to ever be called on. I would sit in fear when they were reading history or whatever they were reading, and they'd call on people to read a paragraph. I mean I would sit there praying, "Don't let her call me, don't let her call me." Because I had to stand up in front of my friends and "Ah, ah,

I don't know this, what is this word? Ah, and ah, ah, you know." And it was torture and they would giggle. It was humiliating and embarrassing and you didn't know why, and the teacher didn't know why. All they knew is you were a slow reader. And of course they had their bluebirds and their blackbirds in there, all that stuff. I was always in the lowest group, you know the blackbirds or whatever. In fifth grade, one of my favorite teachers was Mrs. Shannon, and she took five of us, and while everybody else did work, she sat us in the front of the room, on the floor, and tried to teach us how to read. And instead of finding that embarrassing, I thought, somebody is paying attention to me, this is fun. I'm taken away from the other ones, I don't have to do that work, woo-hoo! And somebody is paying attention to my problem. But the, the incredible thing was, they could teach you to read but you couldn't remember what you read. I could not recall a thing. I would absolutely freeze.

These experiences created an environment in which cheating seemed the only option. I cheated all the time, because I had studied. I knew where it was on the page. I could see it in the book. I knew what column it was in, I knew where the answer was, but I could not bring it into and put it on a test or answer it in any way, and that was so frustrating. But I never knew to say to somebody, "You know what, I studied this." My dad knew I studied. He knew I knew it when he quizzed me that night, but the next day I couldn't spit it out.

Advocating for Your Daughter at School

Sharon recalls a memory that makes her "absolutely shudder":

> I was in about eighth grade and we had to write a speech and give it. So my dad said, "Let's do it on basketball, you know all about basketball, you're a great basketball player, you know the sport, let's do it on that."

Sharon's father intuitively knew that tapping into his daughter's natural abilities and interests would make the task of speech writing and delivery more accessible. What wonderful words of encouragement and praise. This was the fodder for Sharon's self-esteem. Sadly the encouragement stopped here. The day of the speech was disastrous:

> I got up there and I could not say one word, could not remember one word. And I'm telling you, it was so humiliating and the teacher just lambasted me. "You didn't do it did you? You didn't do a speech." And I said, "Yes I did, yes I did, you can ask my dad." I just remember tears burning in my eyes, going and sitting down, being mad at myself, mad at the teacher, and absolutely humiliated.

The role of advocate only begins in elementary school. The pressures of middle school and high school bring new challenges. Sharon began the process of advocating for herself in some nontraditional ways. The recounting of low expectations by the school coupled with questionable decisions on the part of Sharon create a disturbing dyad.

> Then you get into high school and you had the dumb group, the middle group, and the smart ones, and I was always in the dumb group. And they told us, you all can't learn a hundred vocabulary words a week like everybody else, so you only have to learn ten. I

never read—I never had to read a book. Our class was never made to read a book or write a book report. The first book report I ever wrote was when I got into a state university on probation and I—you're not going to believe this. They made us read a book and write a book report. Well I read Mark Twain's [The Celebrated Jumping Frog from Calaveras County]. I changed the frog to being a rabbit and rewrote it and gave it to the teacher, and they never said a word to me for plagiarism. I wrote the exact thing. He evidently had never read it. That was the first book I ever read, and I just picked it up, it was in my house. You know, I didn't know what book to read, and I copied that almost verbatim. I made it be a rabbit instead of a frog. Second book I read was Mark Twain's [The Adventures of Huckleberry Finn], and my boyfriend wrote the book report for me. I think that's why I married him. I didn't know how to write a book report. I'd never done it.

The Power of Desire

Sharon wanted to become a nurse. She was turned down from every school she applied to—eight nursing schools. To make matters worse, the vice principal at her school sent a letter to each school saying "don't take her." A friend called her up and reported that a new 2-year community college was opening and that they had a 2-year nursing school. She applied, and they accepted her over the phone.

Well I got there, and I ran circles around all the women that were in school. They would come and say, "Please come help me make up this bed, there's a patient in it and they've got IVs." Honey I was (snaps fingers) just doing it. I knew how to do it, I was great at it. I had the personality to make the patient feel comfortable. They were smart women, but they were sweating to death with the hands-on stuff, whereas I was knocking them dead with the hands-on stuff.

And my teachers came up to me and said, "We don't understand what's going on with you. You know as much or more than anybody but you can't pass these tests." And so I was working at a local hospital while I was going to school and this doctor, who wanted to be a psychiatrist, was delivering his first baby. He was—his hands were shaking like this, he was so nervous, and I said, "Don't worry about it OK? I'll be there with you, I'll deliver the baby if I have to, but we'll do it together, don't worry, it's going to be OK." He was a wreck. He had no desire to be in an OR or a delivery room. All he wanted to do was sit across a desk from people. Anyway, when I helped him with that, his wife was a psychology teacher at a state university and he said, "Why don't you go to talk to my wife?" And she tested me and she told me that something is wrong with me, in my recall—there wasn't even a name for it. And she said, "You know the material, you can tell it to me, but you can't write it on a paper, you can't put it down." And so my instructors at nursing school started giving me oral exams, without knowing what in the world they were doing because of what this psychologist had said. And they would say, "OK, tell us how do you start an IV?" "Well, first you do an alcohol prep, then you get the needle and you do a tourniquet and blah blah blah." And they'd say, "she knows it," they'd write the answer down. They had no idea what they were doing. I would love to go find them today and tell them. All I know is that I knew how to be a good nurse. I was great at it, I loved it. I couldn't pass the test.

The next challenge came when Sharon had to take the state licensing boards. She had to take the boards three times. Luck was with her because each section of the test was graded independently. If you took a section and passed, that grade was recorded. If you failed a section, you did not have to repeat the whole test. So in the three times she took the test, she was able to pass. Today, the rules have changed. If you fail a section, you must take the entire test over again.

The Rest of the Story

Sharon had nine brothers and sisters. Eleven people lived in a four-bedroom house with two bathrooms.

> Momma had it in our family; it came from Momma. My first brother did not, I did, my second brother had it, my third sister did not. I mean the fourth child did not, Danny did not, Mimi did not, Mark did have it, Barbara had it, and Michael had it. So that's 50–50. It's interesting how those of us that struggled and those of us that didn't. But it hasn't had anything to do with the kind of people we turned out to be, absolutely none. You think it's determining who you are, how smart you are. You think everywhere you go, people are going to ask you what your SAT score was. You think—my SAT score was 680 combined. People would ask about my SATs, you know when you were in college or something. I'd say I don't know, I forget.
>
> You don't forget, not when it's a 640 the first time and a 680 the second time. You, you know real well. And I thought people were going to wonder what you know, grades I made in biology, and then I thought all this was going to be really important in life and it's not. It doesn't have anything to do with who you are. The thing that is huge is your perception of yourself and your parents, how they treat it. Had I been belittled, and if I had been downgraded and made to be—feel small and stuff, but instead, my dad just jumped in and helped me. I'm one of the lucky ones.

Conclusion

As our daughters pass through the classroom doors, they come equipped with linguistic expertise. They have acquired linguistic competence in the phonology, grammar, word meaning, and pragmatics of their culture's language. Educators must ensure that this expertise is acknowledged and utilized as instruction in reading ensues. I am optimistic that professionals will find common ground and establish a civil debate in the interest of furthering knowledge about the complex processes of literacy acquisition. It is essential to set aside the controversies and questions central to the reading wars and strive for ever-improving research and practice. The literacy community must engage in a détente to effect change and help every child become a reader. In the meantime, the responsibility falls in the hands of parents to make sure their daughters can read, an idea explored more deeply in Chapters 5 and 6.

CHAPTER 5

Dyslexia vs. Dysteachia

The professionals from whom you seek help for your struggling daughter may not have the skills or knowledge to provide the help you so desperately need. Faced with this realization, you must arm yourself with information to both teach and advocate for your daughter. Girls who are blessed with efficient processing of text will learn to read in spite of poor teaching. On the other side of the spectrum are the girls who require organized, systematic, efficient instruction by a highly qualified teacher trained in research-based, sequential, multisensory instructional approaches to be successful. The chance of these girls finding their way into the classroom of a teacher who is highly trained to teach reading is slim.

The overriding expectation of the teacher is to produce observable and quantifiable gains of student reading achievement. Each teacher's belief in his or her ability to produce this outcome will determine the instructional course of action selected. The belief in one's capability to organize and execute a course of action to produce predetermined attainments represents the construct of perceived self-efficacy

(Bandura, 1997). The level of perceived self-efficacy will determine the amount of effort put forth in the attainment of instructional goals as well as the level of the perseverance maintained in the face of adversity. Teachers with a high sense of professional efficacy believe in their abilities to motivate and educate even the most difficult student through extra effort and appropriate pedagogy. Conversely, teachers with a low sense of efficacy believe there is little they can do if students are underachieving, unmotivated, and economically challenged.

The responsibilities of the reading teacher require great skill and carry a high risk of negative consequences. Mastery of literacy as process requires that reading teachers understand the overall system of language (Davidson & Snow, 1995). Expertise in phonological awareness, phonemic awareness, comprehension, vocabulary, and fluency provide the foundational components of a successful reading practice. In addition to providing instruction in these essential areas, the reading teacher must also address the confounding effects of motivation, comorbid disorders like ADHD, and linguistic diversity. The reading teacher's perception of the severity of the student's reading difficulties and confounding variables will determine the teacher's perceived level of efficacy and the subsequent intervention provided to that student.

The suggestion that a reading teacher's instructional behavior is better predicted from his beliefs than from the actual consequences of his actions has tremendous implications for the ways in which reading teachers are prepared. At each subsequent grade level, the reading achievement gap widens. The question must be raised as to whether the expectations and beliefs concerning student achievement outcomes vary as result of teacher demographics and context of instruction. If expectations do vary, then the questions of when, where, and how they vary must be considered. The answers to these questions have potential impact on the design of preservice and inservice training for today's K–12 teachers.

In 1987, Dr. Thomas Armstrong coined the word "dysteachia" to refer to children suffering from inappropriate teaching strategies. We must acknowledge that there is dysteachia—that kids have mislearned because they have been mistaught. I've never seen a girl with an IQ in the average range that couldn't be taught to read. They can all be taught to read if you start at the right level, and you provide a sequence that is going to teach reading systematically.

Although various reasons have been suggested for reading problems, inadequate environment and poor reading instruction are at the top of the list. Environmental explanations of poor reading achievement include limited opportunities for adequate oral language development, lack of access to text material in the home, and few parental models of engagement in literacy activities. Instructional limitations include ineffective instructional methods performed by teachers lacking basic knowledge about the reading process.

There has been a tremendous amount of concern that students from high-risk home environments come to school less prepared for literacy than their more advantaged peers. The impact of poorly prepared teachers supersedes high-risk environments as a perpetrator of creating and exacerbating reading difficulties. As a society, we can do little to ameliorate the economic conditions from which many of our girls emerge but we must put a stop to the practice of placing poorly prepared teachers in the critical position of teaching our girls to read. The pervasiveness of this lack of teacher preparation is exemplified by a survey that was administered to 89 reading teachers, special education teachers, and speech-language pathologists (Moats, 1994). Responses to the survey indicated an inadequate understanding of language concepts and persistent weaknesses related to the concepts of the very skills needed for direct, language-focused reading instruction. Furthermore, few of these individuals could identify examples of the basic reading components taught in the primary grades. The conclusion from this survey is that "ignorance was the norm" (Moats, 1994, p. 93).

Several other studies have utilized a similar questionnaire format. For instance, Bos, Mather, Dickson, Podhajski, and Chard (2001) examined the linguistic knowledge of preservice and in-service teachers using two separate questionnaires. The first measured teachers' knowledge of early reading and spelling instruction, and the other measured basic linguistic knowledge. Both preservice and in-service teachers had scores that fell below the 33rd percentile. In-service teachers believed that poor phonemic awareness contributed to early reading failure, but two thirds of the participants could not correctly define phonemic awareness. Preservice and in-service educators indicated that they strongly believed that K–2 teachers should know how to teach phonics, but the same teachers' responses to phonics-based questions indicated that they lacked the basic knowledge necessary to teach phonics. Teachers also overestimated their knowledge of reading and were unaware of what they knew and did not know.

The Dark Ages of Reading Instruction

The term *whole language* describes a number of related teaching programs that swept the world in the 1970s and 1980s. Advocates of whole language share a common belief that learning to read is a natural process similar to learning to speak. If the child failed to read, parents were asked if they were reading to their child, implying that parental neglect was responsible for reading failure because of inadequate modeling. Whole language encouraged children to use book illustrations as a basis for guessing the text or to read to the end of the sentence and then to try to guess any of the words that they couldn't actually read. Publishers and booksellers then reacted by filling their shops with highly illustrated books rather than with books graded from easy-to-difficult text complexity.

Whole language advocates also pointed out that when babies said words like "man," they spoke it as a single unit. They therefore jumped to the conclusions that the traditional phonics practices of teaching sounds, of accurately blending those sounds into syllables, and of blending the syllables into longer words, were not essential to learning to read. Teachers were trained to encourage children to guess words as a whole unit rather than to break the words down into their isolated sounds. Whole language advocates actively discouraged teachers from using any phonics instruction approaches. Teachers were told that if the guess made logical sense, it didn't even matter if it was inaccurate. Forgotten was a focus on the author's meaning and the ultimate true comprehension of text.

Traditional phonics strategies were attacked and almost totally discarded by teacher trainers. This happened, not because of any supportive research, but merely to fit within their preoccupation with word guessing and context cues. Researchers have never been able to demonstrate the efficacy of this guessing approach.

We now know that these whole language advocates were wrong; in fact they have been wrong for three decades. They were only able to maintain their error because the philosophy that spawned whole language included opposition not only to teaching basic phonics skills, but also to testing those skills. By refusing to properly test the outcomes of their practices, educators thereby hid the failure of whole language instruction.

The whole language assertion, that learning to read is the same process as learning to speak, has long been ridiculed by researchers. Speech is a universal, instinctive process; everyone can speak. But reading is not a natural process, it is a learned process. After 4,000 years of learning to read, there are still people on Earth who can speak but cannot read a word. The evidence of failure was there for all to see. Reading is an unnatural process that we challenge the mind to undertake.

One of the leading advocates of whole language guessing practices was Kenneth Goodman. He once described reading as a "psycholinguistic guessing game" and yet, as far back as 1978, Goodman's own university (University of Arizona) demonstrated, in one of the biggest literacy studies ever carried out, that whole language strategies failed in almost every aspect of literacy. The margin of defeat for the whole language method was 14 times that necessary to prove statistical significance. And yet the whole language advocacy continued unabated, impervious to data, driven by belief. Until California, historically the most literate state in the U.S., tested the outcomes.

Californians found that in the years during which whole language had been mandatory in California, the state had slipped from the top to the bottom of the educational literacy league. Other states followed, abandoning the approach, including North Carolina, Ohio, Arizona, Massachusetts, and Texas.

However, many whole language advocates in education departments of universities in the United States still remain in place and in control of teacher training. They still refuse to accept any contrary evidence. Many introductory reading courses have gone to an online format and provide teachers with little more than busy work and an emphasis on critical literacy rather than reading instruction. They do this because this is all they know. University instructors were never taught how to teach a child to read because most are products of the philosophy of whole language instruction. Most left the classrooms themselves and have little hands-on knowledge of how difficult it is to teach a child to read. This is not mere hindsight: Researchers had been issuing warnings right from the outset. The evidence and the science were simply ignored for almost three decades.

Conclusion

You must never forget that the professionals entrusted with helping your struggling daughter may not have the skills or knowledge to provide the help she so desperately needs. As disturbing as this fact is, you must continue to demand appropriately trained professionals who can deliver the research-based, multisensory programs your daughter needs to succeed.

I meet many teachers-in-training and have yet to meet one trainee who has a working knowledge of the linguistic foundations of learning to read. They complain that their literacy classes focus on social justice rather than improvement of literacy skills. It is up to you as parents to fill in the instruction gap with a strong knowledge of how children learn to read, which is where Chapter 6 and the strategies I present for parents to use at home come in.

CHAPTER 6

What Parents Can Do at Home to Increase Reading Abilities

Children follow predictable stages of reading development (Chall, 1983). The typical developmental sequence begins when your daughter realizes that words are made up of a series of sounds and starts to recognize rhyme. If the sequence develops as expected, preschoolers learn to recognize the letters of the alphabet and the sounds associated with letters. As a point of reference, I am including the expected progression through the stages of reading. As with any developmental sequence, precise ages for mastering these milestones are arbitrary. I present them as a point of reference and a means by which to track your daughter's progress.

Developmental Reading Stages

Stage 1: Initial Reading or Decoding Stage (Ages 6–7)

At this stage, your daughter develops an understanding that letters and letter combinations represent sounds. She uses this knowledge to blend together the sounds of phonetically consistent words such as "cat" or "hop." Even though you daughter understands that individual letters represent discrete sounds, she may still find it difficult to segment sounds in an orally presented sound. For example, if you say /cat/, your daughter may have difficulty segmenting that word into the discrete sounds of /c/ /a/ /t/. In addition, she may also have difficulty blending the individual sounds. Both of these skills are prerequisites for the decoding process. As such, decoding is the process by which a word is broken into individual phonemes and blended back together to create a word. Your daughter may reach each of these stages at a later-than-typical age. Keep in mind that your child will need to move through each stage at her own pace.

Stage 2: Confirmation, Fluency, Ungluing From Print (Ages 7–8)

As you daughter begins to develop fluency and additional strategies to gain meaning from print, she is ready to read without sounding everything out. She will begin to recognize whole words by their visual appearance and letter sequence (orthographic knowledge). She will start recognizing familiar patterns and hopefully reach automaticity in word recognition.

Your daughter will need extra repetitions to develop the strategies that lead to fluency. Because your daughter's ability to recognize whole words may be hampered by auditory or visual perceptual problems, as many as 1,000 repetitions may be necessary for mastery of decoding to occur. This is a daunting number. It requires creativity and patience on everyone's part to persevere through this process.

Without commitment to this lengthy and intense process, your daughter will begin to fall seriously behind. Do not expect the classroom instruction to incorporate this level of intervention, as the skills your daughter needs are often not explicitly taught and certainly not extensively practiced.

Stage 3: Reading to Learn (Ages 8–14)

Readers in this stage have mastered the "code" and can easily sound out unfamiliar words and read with fluency. Now they must use reading as a tool for acquiring new knowledge. At this stage, word meaning, prior knowledge, and strategic knowledge become more important.

Your child will need help to develop the ability to understand sentences, paragraphs, and chapters as she reads. Reading instruction should include study of word morphology, roots, and prefixes, as well as a number of strategies to aid comprehension. About 40% of children with reading difficulties have problems that are not apparent until they reach fourth grade.

Stage 4: Multiple Viewpoints (Ages 14–18)

In contrast to the previous stage of reading for specific information, students are now exposed to multiple viewpoints about subjects. They are able to analyze what they read, deal with layers of facts and concepts, and react critically to the different viewpoints they encounter.

When your daughter reaches the phase where reading involves more complex thinking and analysis, she is ready to shine. She may still have difficulty with some of the mechanics of reading, but her mind is well suited to the sharing and manipulation of ideas. She will be well prepared to move on to the final, fifth stage of reading—college level and beyond. If you can successfully guide your daughter through the early stage barriers to this phase, she will be able to excel at understanding and integrating advanced reading material.

Checklist for Gauging Emerging, Early, and Developing Reading Skills

The checklist in Figure 1 can be used as a guide as you work with your daughter at home. The checklist is not sequential in nature. Many of these skills will occur simultaneously. Use the checklist as a guide-post for instruction, as well as assessment as to where your daughter is currently located in the reading continuum.

Essential Components of Reading

Your ability to work with your daughter and help her practice specific reading components can dramatically improve her ability to read. Research shows that there are essential components of reading that must be taught in order to learn to read. You can help your daughter learn to be a good reader by systematically practicing these components:

➤ *Alphabetic principle* is made up of two parts: alphabetic under-standing, or the knowledge that words are made up of letters that represent different sounds, and phonological recoding, or using the relation between those letters and sounds to pro-nounce and spell words (NICHD, 2000).

➤ *Concepts of print* refers to the fundamental principles about reading a book. This includes the basics of how to hold a book to the more abstract concept of what is a "word." The finale occurs with the realization that we combine words into sen-tences to communicate a message.

➤ Recognizing and using individual sounds to create words, or *phonemic awareness*. Your daughter needs to be taught to hear sounds in words and that words are made up of the smallest parts of sound, or phonemes.

➤ Understanding the relationships between written letters and spoken sounds, or *phonics*. Your daughter needs to be taught the sounds that individual printed letters and groups of letters make. Knowing the relationships between letters and sounds

Emerging Reader Checklist

	Engages briefly with books shared one-on-one
	Relies on others to read or share books
	Begins to recognize some letters
	Recognizes her first name
	Recognizes her last name
	Enjoys having books read to her
	Enjoys looking at books on her own
	Repeats words or phrases from familiar books
	Makes up her own story with books
	Identifies some letters
	Identifies most letters
	Has an awareness of environmental print (e.g., signs, logos, cereal boxes)
	Responds to books read to her
	Begins to choose books on her own
	Retells a story by looking at pictures after repeated listening experiences
	Knows how a book progresses from beginning to end
	Knows the difference between a letter and a word
	Identifies all of the letters
	Begins to hear consonant sounds

Early Reader Checklist

	Engages in reading reenactment
	Memorizes some texts
	Shows directionality by running finger along lines of text (left to right and top to bottom)
	Reproduces consonant sounds
	Uses initial consonants to identify words
	Begins to remember a few high-frequency sight words
	Matches print words with spoken words in new text

Figure 1. *Checklist for gauging emerging, early, and developing reading skills.*

Early Reader Checklist, Continued.

	Rereads familiar stories
	Reads self-created written messages
	Retells a familiar story without the book
	Uses pictures as cues when reading text
	Predicts story events, words, and story endings
	Needs encouragement when reading new words or books
	Uses both initial and final consonants to identify words
	Knows what vowels are
	Reads using one-to-one correspondence and self-corrects errors
	Begins to develop fluency with familiar books
	Needs help to select appropriate reading material
	Builds on his or her high-frequency sight word vocabulary
	Uses beginning, middle, and ending consonants to identify words

Developing Reader Checklist

	Discusses and retells story to demonstrate understanding
	Compares or contrasts own experience with story
	Makes connections with other literature
	Reads new text one word at a time but shows some evidence of phrasing
	Corrects most errors that interfere with meaning
	Uses a variety of strategies when reading
	Comments on character, plot, and setting when prompted
	Chooses new as well as previously read books; begins to analyze words and make connections
	Recognizes word family patterns
	Distinguishes small words within a larger word
	Decodes and encodes consonant blends (/tr/, /dr/, /st/)
	Decodes and encodes consonant digraphs (/sh/, /ch/, /th/, /wh/, /ph/)
	Decodes and encodes words with short vowels (cat, hop, sip, cut, get)

Figure 1. *Continued.*

Developing Reader Checklist, Continued.

	Decodes and encodes silent e (like, tape, Pete, cute, hope)
	Identifies y as a vowel
	Decodes and encodes vowel digraphs (rain, way, heal, keep, rein)
	Decodes and encodes diphthongs (au, oi, oy, oo)
	Decodes and encodes prefixes/suffixes
	Decodes and encodes words
	Decodes and spells contractions
	Recognizes high-frequency sight words
	Is moving toward independence
	Reads fluently with expression most of the time
	Recognizes which errors are important to self-correct
	Demonstrates comprehension of reading material through discussion and retelling
	Changes expression and inflection when reading aloud
	Answers and understands written questions
	Uses prior knowledge to make predictions
	Makes good use of reading time and chooses to read
	Selects appropriate reading material
	Views self as reader
	Retells story including setting, sequence of events, main idea, characters, and conclusion
	Reads fluently with proper expression
	Rarely makes mistakes
	Demonstrates higher levels of thinking skills in comprehension of reading material
	Picks up on nuances in books (e.g., humor, sadness, injustice)
	Makes informed predictions using prior knowledge
	Makes connections independently
	Chooses to read for a variety of purposes
	Welcomes challenges as a reader
	Reads a variety of reading material (e.g., fiction, nonfiction, poetry)

Figure 1. *Continued.*

helps children to recognize familiar words accurately and automatically and to decode new words.

➤ Developing the ability to read a text accurately and quickly, or *reading fluency*. Your daughter must learn to read words rapidly and accurately in order to understand what is read. When fluent readers read silently, they recognize words automatically. When fluent readers read aloud, they read effortlessly and with expression. Readers who are weak in fluency read slowly, word by word, focusing on decoding words instead of comprehending meaning.

➤ Learning the meaning and pronunciation of words, or *vocabulary development*. Your daughter needs to actively build and expand her knowledge of written and spoken words, what they mean and how they are used.

➤ Acquiring strategies to understand, remember, and communicate what is read, or *reading comprehension strategies*. Your daughter needs to be taught comprehension strategies, or the steps good readers use to make sure they understand text. Those who are in control of their own reading comprehension become purposeful, active readers.

Alphabetic Principle

The alphabetic principle can be a challenge to many young readers (Snow et al., 1998). The alphabetic principle is made up of two parts: alphabetic understanding, or the knowledge that words are made up of letters that represent different sounds, and phonological recoding, or using the relation between those letters and sounds to pronounce and spell words (NICHD, 2000). The primary difference between good and poor readers is the ability to use letter-sound correspondence to identify words (Juel & Minden-Cupp, 2004). The combination of instruction in phonemic awareness and letter-sound relationships results in your daughter's ability to acquire and apply the alphabetic principle early in her reading career, thus becoming an efficient reader.

Unfortunately, many young children struggle to consistently and automatically identify letters of the alphabet by sight or make the connection between a letter, its name, and its sound. Children who have difficulty making this initial connection often develop difficulties reading words in isolation and in context. They experience a breakdown in developing the alphabetic principle and in learning how to apply this knowledge in their reading (NICHD, 2000). There are several reasons for this breakdown, including the number of associations that beginning readers must learn:

> ➢ There are 40 sounds for 52 random symbols, as well as sounds formed by the combination of these arbitrary symbols (Ehri & McCormick, 2004).
> ➢ The English language uses a system in which the associations between letters and sounds are totally arbitrary, as there is nothing inherent in the visual symbol that suggests its name or sound.
> ➢ Several of the letters in the alphabet are confusing and look alike.
> ➢ Letters challenge the unimportance of spatial orientation. A cup is a cup no matter which way it is turned; however, the letter p can become the letter b, d, or q depending on how it is turned.

The method of instruction may delay the development of the alphabetic principle. Teachers frequently focus on teaching letter names and then introduce the letter sounds under the rationale that the sound of a letter is often similar to its name. However, there are some letter sounds that do not offer consistent clues to the sounds they represent on the basis of their name (e.g., g, c, h). Some children may never make letter-sound connection using this method of instruction.

Teachers typically use their experience, commercial programs and materials, and free interactive websites (e.g., http://www.starfall.com) as interventions. Common activities include alphabet books, games, or forming letters out of clay or Wikki Stix.

Another method for mastering the alphabetic principle is by using integrated picture mnemonics. This involves building a familiar picture around the letter shape. For example, the letter b can be represented through the picture of a bat and baseball, so that the picture name begins with the target sound. Research (de Graaff, Verhoeven, Bosman, & Hasselman, 2007) suggests that prereaders who were taught letter-sound associations through integrated picture mnemonics learned more letter-sound associations than did their peers who were not exposed to the mnemonics. Cardinal Concepts in Education has created a set of integrated alphabet cards with accompanying materials that can be purchased at its website (http://thecardinalconcepts.com).

Alphabetic Principle Activities

The following are some interactive activities parents can use to help their daughters learn alphabetic principles.

- ➢ Fill an empty cookie sheet with flour or rice and let your child trace letters with her fingers. Shake the tin to start over.
- ➢ Fill a large resealable see-through bag with shaving foam. Close it tight (!) and let your daughter use her finger to make letters in the foam.
- ➢ Choose a Letter of the Day or Week. Print out your chosen letter and color it in. Pin it up on a large piece of paper and as your child comes across items, she should write them under the letter or cut out pictures and glue them underneath the letter. You could also turn this into a placemat by laminating the paper.
- ➢ Teach the letter names by singing the alphabet song. Point to the letters on an alphabet chart as you sing so that your daughter can see that the letter names match the printed letters.
- ➢ Make an alphabet book. Give each page a letter of the alphabet, and stick in magazine pictures that begin with the associated letter sound. Let your child read the book with you.
- ➢ Make alphabet placemats. Cut out lots of letters from magazines and glue them onto some cardstock. Laminate and use at meal times so your daughter is constantly exposed to the alphabet.

➤ Make alphabet bookmarks. Write or print the first letter of your child's name onto the top of a blank bookmark. Have her cut out examples of this letter in different fonts from magazines or a picture that begins with this initial letter and glue them on the bookmark. Then, use it with your child's favorite books.

➤ Make alphabet popsicle sticks. Buy 26 popsicle sticks and 26 wood cutouts, such as flowers, that you can glue onto the sticks. With a black permanent marker, mark each cutout with a letter of the alphabet. I made these and played all sorts of games with them. For example, each day the child (or you) can pick a flower to be the letter of the day—then go on a letter hunt around your home to find the letter!

➤ Make or purchase a wall hanging with 26 pockets. Mark each pocket with a letter of the alphabet and put items inside that start with the same letter. (Check out teacher supply stores for ready-made wall hangings.)

➤ Make an alphabet sticker book using purchased stickers. You can get some great ones from craft stores.

➤ Have your child trace her name. Write her name clearly with a black marker on white paper. Tape tracing paper over the paper (this stops the paper from slipping) and let her trace her name with a pencil. This helps her associate the shape of the letters with the letters of her name and is also excellent for those early printing skills. Move on to tracing the rest of the alphabet letters. (You could also have your daughter trace out words she wants to learn, like other family members' or pets' names.)

➤ Buy alphabet beads and have your daughter make her own alphabet necklace, key ring, anklet, or bracelet. She can make these for friends or family members, too, and learn more letters.

➤ Make an A–Z bead snake with beads threaded onto a string. Teach the alphabet song and point to each bead as you sing.

➤ Stencil the alphabet around your daughter's bedroom or onto a piece of furniture or lampshade for her room.

➢ Make tactile letters—use glue to stencil letters onto paper or cardboard and cover them with sand or glitter.
➢ Use alphabet rubber stamps to make decorative cards or bookmarks.
➢ Make some alphabet cookies using letter-shaped cookie cutters, or use the cookie cutters with playdough.

Remember, work for short stretches at a time, as you don't want to frustrate your daughter. Just spend 10–20 minutes each day on the alphabetic principle, and you'll be amazed at her progress.

Apps for Alphabetic Principle

◆ *ABC Shore.* This app is focused specifically on uppercase alphabet/letter recognition. Your daughter is able to use this app independently, so it's perfect on Mom or Dad's iPhone in the backseat of the car. There's no need for parents to adjust settings, worry about advertising or branded characters, or help kids navigate levels. There's also no inappropriate content. It is fun for kids without sacrificing educational benefit—much more enjoyable and likely to be used than flashcard-style "drill 'til you kill" apps.

◆ *Alphabetic.* This is a challenging letter search game, most suitable for slightly older children due to its settings/features and frantic pace. It has a "chat with other players" feature, which makes me nervous and seems out of place in an app for young kids. They also encourage you to buy their other apps from within the app itself.

◆ *Alpha Writer.* This is an app for children that teaches learning to read by forming words. If you teach spelling with phonetics, you'd like this one since it reinforces letter sounds, especially when they're combined. However, it does need a parent's involvement to explain some complex phonemes.

◆ *Dr. Seuss's ABC.* Pricey, but one of the all-time best and most-recognized alphabet apps. It not only emphasizes letters, but also vocabulary, spelling, and picture-word matching. This app has delightful artwork and narration.

◆ *iWriteWords.* This is a fun app, but more focused on writing the alphabet and numbers than learning to recognize them (related but different skills). If kids like "connect the dots"-style tracing, they'll enjoy this one.

◆ *Shape-O ABC's.* This app uses cute puzzles to teach the spelling of simple words. Spelling is a higher order skill than letter recognition, so this app would seem more suitable for a girl with more advanced literacy skills.

◆ *Super Why!* This app is from PBS, so you know it's fun and based on educational research. The app has four games within it, so there's good value for your money. Young girls will like it, and it emphasizes spelling and literacy skills like rhyming and letter writing. Definitely recommended! There are also other Super Why! alphabet games if your daughter likes this one.

Concepts of Print

Concepts of print (also called print concepts) refers to the fundamental principles of reading a book. This includes the basics of how to hold a book to the more abstract concept of what makes a word. The teaching of this concept ends with the realization that we combine words into sentences to communicate a message.

A child needs to know how to hold a book and where to start reading. She must learn to track words left to right and then continue from the end of one line to the beginning of the next line (return sweep). Although these print concepts are obvious to parents, they are not always obvious for your daughter. She will easily grasp these concepts if you read to her every day. Fill your home with books, magazines, and newspapers. This encourages the development of both print concepts and awareness.

Print Concepts Activities

The following are examples of easy and free activities that build the concepts of print:

➢ Visit a local library or used bookstore and show her how to pick up and look at books. Show her how to find the title of the book and, if she's ready, where a description of the book might be located (on the jacket or back).

➢ Write your daughter's name on her possessions.

➢ Point out environmental print such as stop signs, store names, and street signs.

➢ Let your daughter catch you enjoying a good book.

➢ As you read to her, let her hold the book and show her where the story starts and ends.

➢ Let your daughter turn the pages and trace the sentences with her finger as you read.

You can also employ the following specific activities with your child:

➢ *Silly reader.* Hold your daughter's favorite book upside down and ask questions such as "Is this the correct way to hold a book? How do you hold a book?" Using your finger to trace the sentences, read right to left and then ask questions like "Is that backward? How do I read the lines?" Read the illustrations instead of the words and then ask questions such as "Should I be reading the pictures or do I read the words?" Start at the back of the book, with the last word, and begin reading backward, asking more questions.

➢ *Print concepts assessment.* Using the same favorite book, give the following directions and note your child's difficulties.

▪ Show me the cover (front) of the book.

▪ Show me the back of the book.

▪ Point to where I start to read.

▪ Show me which direction I should read each line.

▪ Point to a word. Point to each word as I read it.

▪ Point to a letter.

- Count the words
- Count the letters
- Show me the spaces between words.
- Show me a period, question mark, or comma.

Apps for Print Concepts

◆ *ABC Expedition.* This is an app designed to help children with the alphabet. However, it also helps children learn various animals in the process. This is promised to be a fun app for both parents and kids.

◆ *Alphabytes.* This is an educational app that helps kids learn their letters, the sounds letters make, how to write both upper- and lowercase letters, and how to spell a few words. The game has four sections: Alphabet, Trace, Spell, and Play. Trace teaches kids how to print both upper- and lowercase letters. The Play section of the app has a memory game where kids match letters with the picture of an item that begins with that letter.

◆ *The Electric Company Wordball.* This app incorporates video from the popular television show with a game to teach reading and spelling. The videos are appropriate for any age child learning to read. Kids can listen to some of their favorite music artists as they maneuver through the game. Also, some of the characters from The Electric Company show appear in the game.

◆ *Interactive Alphabet.* This app offers alphabet matching for babies, toddlers, and preschoolers. Your child can hear words, letters, and phonics sounds. It auto advances every 15 seconds. This interactive game teaches upper- and lowercase letters.

◆ *Word Wizard.* This is the first educational app that utilizes natural sounding text-to-speech voices to help kids learn word building and spelling. The Movable Alphabet feature helps kids hear the text they wrote, as well as verify spelling using the built-in spell checker. This app has the ability to turn whatever words kids create—even words that do not exist—into spoken words. This app also includes the most frequently used words, words for body parts, and words for family members, just to name a few.

Phonemic Awareness

Phonemes are the smallest units composing spoken language. For example, the words "it" and "the" each consist of two sounds or phonemes. Phonemes are different from letters that represent phonemes in the spellings of words. Instruction in phonemic awareness involves teaching children to focus on and manipulate phonemes in spoken syllables and words.

The National Reading Panel (2000) reported that phonemic awareness and letter knowledge are the two best predictors of how well children will learn to read. Phonemic awareness provides foundational knowledge in the alphabetic system and is the ability to notice, think about, and work with the individual sounds in spoken words. An example of phonemic awareness is blending and segmenting the separate sounds of a word. For example, when segmenting the sounds of a word, begin by introducing a word orally. You say "cat." Ask your daughter to repeat the word. She says "cat." Explain that you would like her to break the word into separate sounds. Place three coins on the table and model segmenting by moving a coin while saying each sound in the word. For blending, separate the three coins on the table. Select a new three-letter word and isolate each sound while touching a coin. Move the coins closer and say each sound in sequence, increasing your speed as you move the coins closer and closer together until your daughter can successfully blend the word.

Although phonemic awareness is a widely used term in reading, it is often misunderstood. One misunderstanding is that phonemic awareness and phonics are the same thing. Phonemic awareness is the understanding that the sounds of spoken language work together to make words. Phonics is the understanding that there is a relationship between letters and sounds through written language. If girls are to benefit from phonics instruction, they need phonemic awareness. This is because girls who cannot hear and work with the phonemes of spoken words will have a difficult time learning how to relate these phonemes to letters when they see them in written words. Make the activities listed below fun and exciting. Play with sounds. Exaggerate the sounds and emphasize sounds in different positions; initial position

(/t/ in take) is easiest, then final position (/l/ in bill), with medial position (/ĭ/ in hit) being the hardest.

Phonemic Awareness Activities

Using Elkonin sound boxes. One technique employed to build phonemic awareness is Elkonin boxes. These are three or more adjacent boxes drawn on paper or white board. To get started using these boxes, do the following:

- ➢ Have your daughter draw three boxes on a sheet of paper or dry erase board.
- ➢ Distribute counters to your daughter (counters can be any single object like small cards, coins, or bean bags). Have her place counters above the boxes. Model the activities before she begins.
- ➢ Say a three-letter word. For each phoneme, your daughter moves a counter to each box in a left-to-right progression.
- ➢ For example, you tell her, "Say the word let." She moves the counters to represent the sounds she hears in the word: /l/ /e/ /t/. She says the word again, sliding her finger below the boxes from left to right

Other activities for Elkonin boxes include the following:

- ➢ Ask your daughter to listen for a certain sound in a word. You should then say a word that has that sound. Your daughter places a counter in the first box if she hears the sound in the beginning of the word, in the middle box if she hears the sound in the middle of the word, and in the last box if she hears it at the end of the word. For example, "Listen for the /m/ sound in the following word. Place a counter in the first box if you hear the /m/ sound at the beginning of the word; place a counter in the middle box if you hear the sound in the middle of the word; or place it in the last box if you hear the /m/ sound at the end of the word. Listen carefully. The word is /ham/."

➢ Replace the counters with several letters after appropriate letter-sound correspondences have been introduced. Take the letters a, l, p, s, and n, and have your daughter place or write the corresponding letters in the boxes for the phonemes as you say words. For example, say, "Lap. The cat sat in my lap." Letter magnets or flash cards could also work well here.

➢ Have your daughter write letters in the boxes as you dictate words (Blachman, Ball, Black, & Tangle, 2000). For example, say, "Spell the word big. The big dog barked at the squirrel. Big: /b/ /i/ /g/."

➢ Make colored circles or use colored blocks. Have dry erase pens and a predetermined word list available to read to your daughter. For example, you could pronounce each of the following words one at a time: hat, pet, sit, fish, chip, dot, cup. Ask your daughter to repeat each word. Have her count the number of phonemes in the word, not necessarily the number of letters, by tapping or clapping each sound. For fish, tap /f/, /i/, /sh/. Direct your daughter to slide one colored circle or colored block in each cell of the Elkonin box diagram as she repeats the word. For example, fish has three phonemes and will use three boxes. She will say /f/, /i/, /sh/ as she slides the circles into each box.

Sequences of sounds. Sequential memory is the ability to distinguish and recall items in a particular order. Sequential memory is both auditory, or sound-based, and visual. People with dyslexia can experience difficulty with sequential memory. Use simple activities to develop your daughter's sequential memory, then progress to more challenging activities as her confidence and competence increases. Begin by collecting objects that make interesting and distinctive sounds. Ask your daughter to cover her eyes with her hands while you make a familiar noise such as closing the door, sneezing, or playing a key on the piano. By listening carefully and without peeking, she is to try to identify the noise.

Once she understands the game, try two noises, one after the other. She will then identify the two sounds in sequence. Add the number of sounds in the sequence until her memory load is exhausted. Some noises you might use include:

> ➤ blowing a whistle,
> ➤ clapping,
> ➤ coughing,
> ➤ crumpling paper,
> ➤ drumming with fingers,
> ➤ hammering,
> ➤ ringing a bell,
> ➤ sharpening a pencil,
> ➤ slamming a book,
> ➤ snapping fingers,
> ➤ tearing paper, or
> ➤ whistling.

Name the nonsense. Recite or read aloud a familiar text, changing its words or wording. Your daughter should raise her hand whenever changes occur. You can change phonemes, words, grammar, and meaning. In addition, you can swap word order, word parts, and order of events. Here are some examples of the "nonsense" that can be created within familiar phrases and rhymes:

> ➤ Once a time upon . . . (reversed words)
> ➤ The little red caboose always came first (substitute words)
> ➤ Twinkle, twinkle little car . . . (substitute words)

Clapping names. When you first introduce this activity, model it by using several names of contrasting lengths. Pronounce the first names of family members syllable by syllable while clapping them out. Then ask your daughter to say and clap the name along with you. Explain that each clap represents a syllable or word part. After each name has been clapped, ask her, "How many syllables did you hear?" If she has difficulty counting syllables, have her hold two fingers horizontally under her chin, so she can feel her chin drop for each syllable. Placing her hand on her throat will allow your daughter to feel the vibration of each syllable.

Initial phoneme sort. Create picture cards using magazines or computer clip art. Paste the pictures on index cards and laminate if possible. Spread selected pictures in front of your daughter. Then ask her to find the picture whose name starts with a selected initial phoneme.

As each picture is found, she will name the picture and the initial phoneme. For example, you can ask: "What picture begins with the sound /r/?" She might respond: "Ruler. /r/."

Initial phoneme sort advanced. Group the phonemes into sets of three. Collect multiple picture cards for the three distinct phonemes For example, start with the phonemes /t/, /m/, and /f/. Group phonemes that are easily distinguishable. Avoid grouping phonemes such as /v/ and /f/ or /b/ and /p/ because of their sound and formation similarities. As your daughter becomes more competent in distinguishing speech sounds, you may then begin to incorporate more challenging groupings. Place the picture cards in front of your daughter. She will then sort them based on their common initial consonant sound. If three phonemes prove to be too difficult, adjust the cards to represent two initial phonemes.

Phoneme substitution. In this oral activity, your daughter will make new words by replacing the first sound in the word with the target sound. For example, target the phoneme /s/. Ask your daughter to substitute the /h/ in "hand" with /s/. She should respond with "sand." Some additional words to use with the targeted /s/ phoneme are: "hit," "well," "funny," "bun," "mad," "bend," and "rat." With the substitution of /s/ in the initial position the words become "sit," "sell," "sunny," "sad," "sun," "send," and "sat."

Secret code. This is a technique for building phonemic awareness in which your daughter listens to a sequence of separately spoken phonemes (e.g., /b/ /a/ /t/), then combines them to form a single word ("bat"). You will need picture cards with pictures of words containing three or four sounds. Blending sounds is the process of smoothly joining phonemes to come up with a pronunciation close enough to a word to access the word. A simple blending activity is Secret Code, a guessing game. Turn a picture card face down and name its phonemes (e.g., /h/ /a/ /t/). When your daughter blends the phonemes and guesses the word, you show her the picture. You also have the option of bringing out the Elkonin boxes. While pointing to each box, your daughter must repeat the phonemes /h/ /a/ /t/ over and over and faster and faster until she knows the identity of the picture.

What's my secret picture? Place multiple picture cards in a bag or box. Select a picture from the bag. Explain that you have a secret picture, and you will give a hint by saying the sounds that make up the name of your secret. Say, "I will name my secret pictures in sounds and when you figure out what it is, it will be your turn." Pronounce the name of the secret picture phoneme by phoneme. For a picture of a cat, you will say /c/ /a/ /t/. When your daughter guesses the word "cat," she gets the card. Then she should draw a picture and name a secret word for you. In this way she gets practice in blending and segmenting phonemes. Work up from short (two- and three-sound) words to longer ones as your daughter becomes more adept at hearing the sounds. Examples of secret pictures include the following: ape, bean, book, bow, bread, brick, broom, cheese, desk, dog, and dress.

Phonics—The Relationship Between Written and Spoken Letters and Sounds

The National Reading Panel, composed of experts in the field of literacy, was asked by the United States Congress to determine what the research said about the teaching of phonics. To ensure the soundness of its findings, the National Reading Panel (2000) chose to review only studies that met rigorous criteria for research studies. They concluded that phonics is an essential ingredient in beginning reading instruction and found that:

➤ Systematic and explicit phonics instruction—phonics instruction that is direct and follows a particular sequence—is more effective than phonics instruction that is not systematic or no phonics instruction at all.

➤ Systematic, explicit phonics instruction is most effective when it begins in kindergarten or first grade.

> ➤ Systematic, explicit phonics instruction improves children's word recognition, spelling, and reading comprehension skills.
> ➤ Systematic, explicit phonics instruction benefits all children, regardless of their socioeconomic status.
> ➤ Systematic, explicit phonics instruction most benefits children who are having difficulty learning to read.

Phonics instruction is only one part of a complete reading program for beginning readers. Effective beginning reading programs should also emphasize reading fluency, vocabulary development, and text comprehension. Phonics instruction emphasizes letter-sound relationships and their use in reading (decoding) and spelling (encoding). The primary focus of phonics instruction is to help beginning readers understand how letters are linked to sounds (phonemes) to form letter-sound relationships and spelling patterns and to help them learn how to apply this knowledge in their reading of text.

Types of Phonics Instructional Methods and Approaches

Phonics instruction varies relative to the explicitness by which the phonic elements are taught. Many synthetic phonics approaches use direct instruction in teaching phonics and then provide practice in decodable text formats that focus on the skills being taught. Embedded phonics approaches are typically less explicit and use decodable text for practice less frequently.

Systematic phonics instruction produces significant benefits for students in kindergarten through sixth grade and for children having difficulty learning to read. The ability to read and spell words is enhanced in kindergartners who received systematic beginning phonics instruction. First graders who are taught phonics systematically are better able to decode and spell, and they showed significant improvement in their ability to comprehend text. Older children receiving phonics instruction are better able to decode and spell words and to read text orally.

Across all grade levels, systematic phonics instruction improved the ability of good readers to spell. The effects of systematic early phonics instruction are significant and substantial in kindergarten and the first grade, indicating that systematic phonics programs should be implemented at those age and grade levels. Explicit, systematic phonics instruction is a valuable and essential part of a successful reading program. Remember, it is critical to understand that the prerequisite to phonics instruction is phonemic awareness. Your daughter needs to be able to blend spoken sounds together and break spoken words into their individual sounds to be successful in phonics instruction.

There are several different types of phonics instructional approaches that vary according to the unit of analysis or how letter-sound combinations are represented to the student.

Analogy phonics. Teaching students unfamiliar words by analogy to known words, or recognizing that the rime segment of an unfamiliar word is identical to that of a familiar word, and then blending the known rime with the new word onset, such as reading *brick* by recognizing that –ick is contained in the known word kick, or reading *stump* by analogy to the word jump.

Analytic phonics. Teaching students to analyze letter-sound relationships in previously learned words to avoid pronouncing sounds in isolation.

Embedded phonics. Teaching students phonics skills by embedding phonics instruction in text reading. This is a more implicit approach that relies to some extent on incidental learning.

Phonics through spelling. This technique involves teaching students to segment words into phonemes and to select letters for those phonemes (i.e., teaching students to spell words phonemically).

Synthetic phonics. Teaching students explicitly to convert letters into sounds (phonemes) and then blend the sounds to form recognizable words.

Phonics Terminology

To understand written material about phonics, parents should be familiar with the following terms: vowels, consonants, consonant blends (or clusters), consonant digraphs, vowel digraphs, and diphthongs. Each of these are explained below in more detail.

Vowels. The letters a, e, i, o, and u represent vowel sounds, and the letters w and y take on the characteristics of vowels when they appear in the final position in a word or syllable. The letter y also has the characteristics of a vowel in the medial (middle) position in a word or syllable.

Consonants. Letters other than vowels generally represent consonant sounds. W and y have the characteristics of consonants when they appear in the initial position in a word or syllable.

Consonant blends (or clusters). Two or more adjacent consonant letters whose sounds are blended together, with each individual sound retaining its identity, constitute a consonant blend. Consonant blends (also called consonant clusters) are groups of two or three consonants in words that each make a distinct consonant sound, such as /bl/ or /spl/. Consonant blends include:

/bl/	/gl/	/sn/
/br/	/gr/	/sp/
/cl/	/pr/	/st/
/cr/	/sc/	/sw/
/dr/	/sk/	/tr/
/fl/	/sl/	/tw/
/fr/	/sm/	

Some three-letter consonant blends are:

/nth/	/shr/	/squ/
/sch/	/spl/	/str/
/scr/	/spr/	

For example, although the first three sounds in the word strike are blended smoothly, listeners can detect the separate sounds of /s/, /t/, and /r/ being produced in rapid succession. Other examples are the /spl/ in splash, the /fr/ in frame, the /cl/ in click, and the /br/ in bread, to mention a few. Many teaching materials refer to these letter combinations as consonant clusters rather than consonant blends. The Enchanted Learning site (http://www.enchantedlearning.com/

consonantblends) has examples of words beginning with consonant blends, as well as many great activities and worksheets.

Consonant digraphs. Two adjacent consonant letters that represent a single speech sound constitute a consonant digraph. For example, /sh/ is a consonant digraph in the word shore, because it represents one sound and not a blend of the sounds of s and h. Other consonant digraphs include:

/ch/	/ng/	/th/
/gh/	/ph/	/wh/
/kn/	/sh/	/wr/

Vowel Digraphs. Two adjacent vowel letters that represent a single speech sound constitute a vowel digraph. In the word foot, /oo/ is a vowel digraph.

Diphthongs. Vowel sounds that are so closely blended that they can be treated as single vowel units for the purposes of word identification are called *diphthongs*. When creating a diphthong sound, one has to move the mouth from one position to another. For example, when making the /ow/ sound, the person begins by opening the mouth wide and then changing it to a small circle. Although all diphthongs do not require a change of mouth position, most do.

These sounds are actually vowel blends, because the vocal mechanism produces two sounds instead of one. Diphthongs include:

/aw/	/ou/	/oi/
/au/	/ow/	/oy/

Multisensory Teaching Methods

Samuel T. Orton pioneered the study of learning disabilities. He is best known for his work examining the causes and methods of treatment for dyslexia, including the Orton-Gillingham method. Orton's (1919) study of reading difficulties in children led him to hypothesize that "these individuals have failed to establish appropriate cerebral organization to support the association of visual words with their spoken forms" (p. 286).

The Orton-Gillingham method is the grandfather of structured, sequential, multisensory teaching of written language. It is based upon the use of association as to how a letter or word looks, how it sounds, and how the speech organs feel when producing it. Also incorporated are the common rules of the English language. Older students are challenged to learn syllable patterns, common prefixes and suffixes, and Latin and Greek word parts. (See http://www.orton-gillingham.com for more information.) The Orton-Gillingham method has spawned many variations for teaching phonics. These include the Slingerland Approach, The Spalding Method, Project Read, Alphabetic Phonics, The Herman Method, and the Wilson Reading System. In addition, other approaches incorporate aspects of Orton's work. Examples of the modified approaches are the Sequential English Education and Starting Over.

Two additional well-known intervention models are the Association Method and the Lindamood-Bell methods. Both of these are based on research that has involved hearing- and language-impaired individuals. We will take a look at each method, keeping in mind that to implement any of these methods you have two choices. First, you can use the contact information to find a trained tutor in your area. Second, you can decide to be trained yourself. Each organization has its own requirements for becoming certified. Often, an internship is involved. Materials can be purchased with or without training. Being trained yourself will involve a large initial investment and a great deal of commitment, but will save you much money in the long run.

> *Alphabetic Phonics.* This methodology evolved directly from Orton-Gillingham and combines the auditory learning modality for spelling, the visual modality for reading, and the kinesthetic modality for handwriting. Materials include the Instant Spelling Deck (used for a daily 3-minute drill that focuses on the most probable spelling of each of the 44 speech sounds) and the Initial Reading Deck (a set of 98 cards with picture key words that are chosen by students and are used to teach each of the 44 speech sounds). Assessments provide a record of students' progress in reading, spelling, handwriting, and alphabetizing. For more information, contact School

Specialty at 800-225-5750 or visit the store online at http://www.eps.schoolspecialty.com.

➢ *The Association Method.* The Association Method incorporates multisensory teaching, the teaching of sound/symbol relationships for reading, and the use of cursive writing for initial instruction. Children still learn to read manuscript type, but write only in cursive. Unique to this method is that a slower temporal rate of speech is used to provide children more time to process words auditorily and more time to observe the speaker's lip movements. Precise articulation is required from the beginning. Colors are used to differentiate phonemes within words and to highlight verbs and new concepts in language structures. An individual notebook is created for each child to document what has been learned. For more information, contact The DuBard School for Language Disorders at the University of Southern Mississippi at 601-266-5223 or visit the center's website at http://www.usm.edu/dubard.

➢ *The Herman Method.* This sequence of instruction starts each student at her point of deficit and sequentially teaches her mastery of each skill level. Expansion of each skill occurs vertically and horizontally as in an inverted pyramid. A combination of visual, auditory, kinesthetic, and tactile stimuli help each child compensate for visual and auditory processing problems. All exercises are carefully sequenced and each activity is repeated until automaticity is reached. The Herman Method provides support in decoding and encoding skills, sight word recognition, structural analysis, use of contextual clues, dictionary skills, and comprehension skills. For more information or to purchase materials, visit http://www.soprislearning.com/cs/Satellite/New_Herman_Method_Overview?cmsid=Sopris.

➢ *Lindamood-Bell methods.* One of the Lindamood-Bell methods is The Lindamood® Phonemic Sequencing program (LiPS). LiPS is designed to stimulate phonemic awareness. Children focus on the mouth actions that produce speech sounds. They use this awareness to verify sounds within words. This allows them to become self-correcting in reading, spelling, and speech.

Another methodology is The Visualizing and Verbalizing for Language Comprehension and Thinking (V/V). The V/V program develops concept imagery through a precise series of steps that begin with expressive language and then extend from a word to paragraphs with images. For more information, contact Lindamood-Bell Learning Process at 800-233-1819 or visit the store online at http://www.lindamoodbell.com.

➢ *Project Read.* Project Read provides an alternative approach to teaching reading and written expression concepts and skills in mainstream classrooms as well as in special education. In its initial form, Project Read was limited to being a decoding/encoding program. As it became apparent that students had more pervasive language learning problems, the program was expanded to include reading comprehension and written expression. For more information, contact Language Circle Enterprises and Project Read at 800-450-0343 or visit the company's website at http://www.projectread.com.

➢ *Sequential English Education.* The Sequential English Education (SEE) program is a multisensory structured language approach to teaching reading, writing, and spelling for struggling readers. The initial phase emphasizes the mastery of the code of the English language as well as the alphabetic and phonetic system. It is age appropriate for 5- and 6-year-old children and instruction should be one-on-one or in small groups of no more than 7 students. The SEE program uses a textured memory board for a visual-auditory-tactile-kinesthetic input of new material. Comprehension skills are sequential and begin with word meanings and progress to sentence paraphrasing. For more information, contact The Sequential English Education Training Program at The June Shelton School and Evaluation Center at 214-352-1772 or visit the school's website at http://www.shelton.org.

➢ *The Slingerland Approach.* The Slingerland Approach was developed for preventive instruction. Today it is used both as a preventive and remedial approach. Delivery of the method can occur in classrooms, in small groups, and in one-to-one settings. It is appropriate for students ranging from primary grade to adults. Oral expression, decoding, reading comprehension, spelling, handwriting, and written expression are all taught with the integrated direct instructional approach. Guided practice of these skills supports the goal of independent reading and written expression. For more information, contact the Slingerland Institute for Literacy, One Bellevue Center at 425-453-1190 or visit the organization's website at http://www.slingerland.org.

➤ *The Spalding Method.* This method is delivered as integrated, multisensory instruction in listening, speaking, writing, spelling, and reading. The Spalding principles guide lesson plans, instruction, and decisions. These principles assert that learning should be child-centered and multisensory. In addition, learning should encourage higher level thinking, produce quality work, recognize the value and importance of tasks, and integrate language arts into all curriculum areas. For more information, contact Spalding Education Foundation at 623-434-1204 or visit the organization's website at http://www.spalding.org.

➤ *Starting Over.* This instructional approach is multifaceted in that it includes diagnosis and remediation of decoding, spelling, vocabulary, writing, handwriting, and reading comprehension. The program is based on the belief that dyslexic children and adults can learn to read, spell, and write if they are diagnosed and taught using a multisensory, structured language approach. In addition, teachers can be taught to do both the diagnosis and the remediation. Most significant is the belief that dyslexics can be taught to overcome their difficulty of distinguishing the differences among sounds, thus leading to the capacity to easily decode text and then ultimately move to comprehension. For more information, contact Starting Over at 212-769-2760 or visit the website at http://www.knighteducation.com

➢ *The Wilson Reading System.* The Wilson Reading System is a 12-step remedial reading and writing program for individuals with a language-based learning disability. This program is based on the Orton-Gillingham philosophy and principles and current phonological coding research. The power of this method rests in the fact that it teaches the structure of words so that students master the coding system for reading and spelling. The language system is presented in a simple, systematic, and cumulative manner. This makes it manageable for a young child as well as an adult. Visualization techniques are used for comprehension. For more information, contact Wilson Language Training at 800-899-8454 or visit the company's website at http://www.wilsonlanguage.com.

Phonics Rules and Activities

There are six syllable types. It is very helpful for struggling readers to be able to identify the syllable types in words when trying to read or spell. The sound a vowel makes often depends upon what type of syllable it is in. The following pages provide activities for each syllable type that can be implemented at home or suggested to your daughter's teacher.

CVC rule. If a single vowel is surrounded by consonants, then it usually has a short sound. For example in the word cat, the vowel /ă/ is surrounded by consonants. I often will teach this as the "bully rule." The consonants put the "squeeze" on the vowel thus forcing it to say its shortened sounds. Figure 2 includes a chart of the vowels and sample CVC words.

Word sort for word families. Select three word families and write one CVC word for each. Let's begin with the word families /it/, /ip/, and /ill/. Next, write "will," "sit," and "zip" on index cards. These will be your anchor words. Put these anchor words on the table. Make 10 additional word cards for each word family.

Demonstrate how to isolate each sound by tapping it on your arm. If the child is right handed, the first sound is tapped on the left shoulder, the middle sound is tapped on the left elbow, and the final

Vowels	CVC Words
/a/	bat, cat, tag
/e/	get, den, hem
/i/	hit, lip, pin
/o/	hop, dog, top
/u/	bug, hut, sun

Figure 2. *CVC words.*

sound is tapped on the left wrist. If the child is left handed, the first sound is tapped on the right wrist, the middle sound is tapped on the right elbow, and the final sound is tapped on the right shoulder. This maintains the left to right tracking of text. After demonstrating the technique, have your daughter model the tapping procedure with the anchor words for each word family. Go to your additional word card stack and pick up another word. Model the tapping procedure, then ask your daughter to place the card under the appropriate header. You may need to repeat the tapping of the header words. Once all of the words are sorted, have your daughter read all of the words using the tapping technique as needed. After doing this sort with your daughter, use other common word families to create more sorts. Each sort should be kept in a zipper bag and labeled with the sort criteria. Keep these available for independent work.

CVCe rule. This pattern is often described as the "magical e" rule. If the e is at the end of a word, it signals to the reader that the preceding vowel says its alphabet name or long sound. When a one-syllable word has an e at the end and a vowel in the middle, the first vowel is usually long and the e is silent. In working with students, I continue the bully metaphor and describe the silent e at the end of the CVCe word as the strong silent hero that makes the consonant bullies release their hold on the vowel and, in doing so, allows the vowel to say its alphabet name or long vowel sound. Create a stack of word cards with the following header words as your guide: make, male, pane. These word cards will be used in the following activities:

> *Regular sort.* This is your daughter's opportunity to begin exploring and categorizing the words in her sort by creating

columns or groups of words just as she did with CVC words. Again, use word families to create your sorts. Follow the same instructional procedures as you did with CVC words.

➤ *Blind sort.* Your daughter sorts 10–12 words without the header words. She must discover the rule for sorting.

➤ *Speed sort.* A speed sort is my favorite. Using a stopwatch, your daughter can see how fast she can correctly sort her words.

➤ *Word hunt.* In this sort, select a magazine or newspaper and search for words that fit into a designated sort.

➤ *PowerPoint fun.* Take the words used in previous sorts and create a PowerPoint file with one word on each slide. Your daughter will read the word off the slide. Set the slide transition time at 5-second intervals and decrease the time as your daughter improves. This is great for improving word level fluency and automatic decoding.

Vowel team rule. Your daughter might be taught the phrase, "When two vowels go walking, the first vowel does the talking." The first vowel says it name (long vowel sound) and the second vowel is silent. This is true with most vowel pairs, but not for diphthongs. Examples of vowel teams include ee, ea, oa, and ai. Diphthong examples include ou, oi, and ow.

Following the bully metaphor again, the first vowel hires a strong silent vowel bodyguard that releases the hold of the bully consonants and allow the first vowel to say its alphabet name or long sound. Diphthongs are not pure vowel teams. They are two vowel sounds that are so closely blended that they can be treated as single vowel unit. These sounds are actually vowel blends, because the vocal mechanism produces two sounds instead of one. An example of a diphthong is the ou in out.

Draw a man (better known as hangman). Play this game to help your daughter sharpen her vowel team and diphthong spelling and word-decoding skills.

➤ Start the game choosing a word containing the target vowel team or digraph.

➢ Place one dash on the bottom of a piece of paper for each letter of the word chosen.

➢ Draw a box at the top of the paper for drawing the "man."

➢ Have your daughter guess one letter at a time or she can use a turn to guess the entire word or words.

➢ Fill in the letter (everywhere it appears) on the appropriate dash (or dashes) each time your daughter guesses correctly.

➢ Add one body part to the drawing each time the letter chosen is not in the word. Begin by drawing a head, then add eyes, ears, nose, hair, body, legs, and arms.

➢ If she figures out the word before drawing the entire body, she gets a point. Go for 10 points, changing the vowel team or digraph each round.

Make a word square. Draw a square. Divide the square into nine equal parts. Place a vowel team or digraph in the middle box. Place consonants in remaining boxes (see Figure 3 for a completed word square). Using the designated vowel team or digraph, see how many words your daughter can write that use the letters in the square. Give points for the number of words, the longest words, and the hardest words. Set a point goal each time you play.

R-controlled vowels (also called Bossy R). When the letter r follows a vowel, the vowel is usually forced to change its sound. That's why it is called the "Bossy R." In most small words with one vowel in the middle, that vowel has a short vowel sound, as in the words bad, hen, sit, fox, and fun. The sound of the vowel changes if we replace the last letter of each of these words with the letter r. For example, bad changes to bar, hen to her, sit to sir, fox to for, and fun to fur. The sound /ar/ is usually spelled with the letters ar and /or/ is usually spelled or. The sound /er/ can be spelled with the vowels i, e, or u preceding the letter r. The Word Way Bossy R website (http://www.wordway.us.com/BossyR.htm) provides great examples of the Bossy R in action, along with word lists you can use in the activities that follow.

Bossy R concentration. Make two copies of r-controlled vowel word cards, preferably on cardstock, heavy paper, or index cards. Cut out the word cards and select 40 cards (20 pairs). Be sure to include

s	t	h
r	ea	c
m	p	k

Figure 3. *Sample word square.*

some words from each of the five r-controlled vowel combinations (/ar/, /er/, /ir/, /or/, /ur/).

1. Place the selected cards face down on the table and mix them up.
2. Arrange the face-down cards into rows on the table.
3. You and your daughter take turns flipping over two cards at a time. As the cards are being flipped up, read the words aloud. If a match is made, keep the pair of cards and take another turn. If another match is made, keep the pair of cards and take another turn. If a match is not made, return the cards face down on the table, and it's the other person's turn. See how well you can remember where the cards are placed!
4. When all of the cards on the table have been matched, count your pairs. The player with the most pairs wins.

Open syllable. An open syllable ends in a vowel. The vowel has a long vowel sound, as in the first syllable of apron. You want to begin with high-frequency open syllable words such as me, he, she, we, the, and go. Avoid rule exceptions such as to and do at this point. Continue the bully metaphor and explain that the bullies left the back door open so the vowel can say its name.

Open syllable activities. Two activities that can easily be made at home require construction paper and glue. In the first activity, cut out a house and decorate it with your daughter's help. Cut out an off-center door that can swing open and closed. To the left of the door paste the letters that make an open syllable when the door is open. An example would be to paste the word "go" to the left of the door when the door is open. Behind the open door paste a consonant that will create a closed syllable when the door is closed. For this example use the consonant *t*. With the door open, the word is "go"; with the door closed, the word is "got." Sets of these are fun to make with your daughter and then put in an area where she can work independently.

A second activity for working with open syllables requires a transparent ruler and a list of two-syllable words containing both open and closed initial syllables. Examples of two-syllable words with an initial open syllable could include rodent, minus, tulip, begin, and station. Examples of two-syllable words with an initial closed syllable could include muffin, helmet, letter, and contact. Take the transparent ruler and place it so it covers the first word. We'll use the word begin as an example. Slide the ruler to the left until the first vowel is uncovered. With our example of begin, the ruler will uncover the syllable "be," leaving "gin" under the ruler, but still visible. Ask your daughter to tap the first syllable, focusing on the fact that it is an open syllable and the e is making its long sound. She then needs to tap the syllable left under the transparent ruler and determine if she has made a real word. In this case she has, so she will draw a line indicating the appropriate syllable division. If she does not create a real word, she then slides the ruler over to the left, revealing the next consonant. With the word muffin, she would determine that the first syllable is not open because a real word is not made. Once the ruler slides over and uncovers the letter f and creates the closed syllable "muf," then a real word is made and she makes the correct syllable division. Continue with the rest of the list.

Consonant (C-le). This syllable is found in words like handle, puzzle, and middle. The e is silent and the consonant + l are pronounced like a blend. Also known as the stable final syllable, consonant-le combinations are found only at the ends of words. If a C-le syllable is combined with an open syllable—as in cable, bugle, or title—there is no doubled consonant. If one is combined with a closed syllable—as in dabble, topple, or little—a double consonant results. Not every consonant is found in a C-le syllable. These are the ones that are used in English:

-ble (bubble)   -cle (cycle)   -ckle (trickle)

Closed Syllable	Open Syllable
cattle	fable
hassle	gable
bubble	able
babble	bugle
paddle	rifle
scrabble	idle

Figure 4. *Closed and open syllable words for sorting.*

-dle (riddle)	-kle (wrinkle)	-stle (whistle)
-fle (rifle)	-ple (quadruple)	-tle (whittle)
-gle (bugle)	-sle (hassle)	-zle (puzzle)

Word sort. This activity is a traditional word sort in which your daughter is asked to sort words that all have the consonant-le pattern, but some begin with an open syllable and others begin with a closed syllable. Review these two syllable types before beginning. Words for sorting might include those in Figure 4. Make and cut out your word cards and provide a header (open or closed) for each category. Provide help as needed.

Divide and conquer. Using the same word list, ask your daughter to highlight the consonant-le in each word. Once highlighted, she will then separate the highlighted syllable using a slash mark (no/ble). Have her identify the first syllable as open or closed and then pronounce the word.

PowerPoint fun. Take the words from the chart and create a PowerPoint file with one word on each slide. Your daughter reads from the slides. Set the slide transition time at 5-second intervals and decrease the time as your daughter improves. This is great for improving word level fluency and automatic decoding.

Apps for Phonics

◆ *ABC Phonics Rocks!* ABC Phonics Rocks! teaches students their letter sounds. On the "Letters" section of the game, it displays

128

the alphabet (in capital letters), and when students touch a letter, its sound is produced. On the "Words" section of the game, the student is shown a picture of a simple word to spell, such as hat, and blank spaces are provided for the student to fill in letters to spell the word. When the student touches a space, she hears the phoneme that goes there, and then can choose the corresponding letter to go in that spot. Once the child spells the word correctly, the word dances to music as a reinforcement tool. This app is limited by the fact that only capital letters are used and the sound quality is somewhat limited.

◆ *ABC Pocket Phonics*. ABC Pocket Phonics has two games. In the first game, the student is shown a letter, hears its sound, and is then asked to trace the letter. The tracing task models the correct directionality of letter formation and then gives the child feedback about whether she traced the letter correctly. In the second game, the narrator says a phoneme and asks the child to select the corresponding letter. Then the narrator says the next sound in the word until the whole word is spelled. After all of the letters are chosen, the narrator models blending of the new word. Most of the words are simple CVC words with short vowels.

◆ *Build a Word*. This is a letter-matching game that doesn't teach children how to create words themselves. Build a Word displays a letter on the screen, and then the child must choose the matching letter from a variety of floating letters. The narrator says the letter name, then displays the next letter in the word until the student has matched all of the letters in the word. The student then blends the letters together to make a word. The drawback for this app is that the number of words the child is able to build is very limited.

◆ *Clifford's BE BIG With Words*. This app is centered on a story: Clifford's friend Jetta is painting and needs ideas for what to paint. Below an art easel, the student can choose from 2–4 capital letters to give Jetta some ideas for words to be painted. The student drags and drops any letter she wants into each slot. The game is designed so there is no chance the child will produce a nonword. Once the three slots are filled, the narrator sounds out each letter and then says, "You spelled ___!" This app is limited by the fact that it says the letter sound instead of the letter name when the student is dragging and dropping each letter onto the easel. However, this app is great reinforcement for students who are learning to spell simple CVC (consonant-vowel-consonant) words with short vowels.

◆ *Doodle Buddy.* In this app, the student uses her finger to draw on the screen. As she draws, she has options to change the color of the paint and the size of the crayon. Doodle Buddy is a great app for adding a multisensory component to a variety of skill-based lessons. There is an option to save completed pictures into iPhoto, which can then be transferred to your computer, printed, and added to your daughter's portfolio. This is a great app for reluctant writers who balk at using paper and pencil. This new dynamic is a true motivator.

◆ *The Phonics Made Easy Flash Action.* Phonics Made Easy Flash Action app has been developed to help children sharpen important phonics skills for reading success. In using this app, children will explore beginning and ending letter sounds, recognize long and short vowel sounds, familiarize themselves with rhyming families, and work with letter blends. Audio within the app makes phonic skills much easier to learn, when children can hear letter sounds while working.

Fluency

Good readers read quickly, effortlessly, and with automaticity. When a task that formerly required attention for its performance can be performed without attention, the task is being done automatically. Automaticity in information processing, then, simply means that information is processed with little attention. One way to determine if a person is performing a process automatically is to give him or her two tasks to perform at the same time. If the tasks can be performed simultaneously, then at least one of them is being done automatically. When a fluent reader reads aloud, she reads with tone and expression, inserting appropriate pauses and emphasizing appropriate words. If children labor to decode words, then they do not have attention or mental resources left over to dedicate to comprehension and enjoyment.

According to the National Reading Panel (2000), fluency is the ability to read a text quickly, accurately, and with proper expression. If individuals are low in fluency, they also will have difficulty with comprehension. The National Reading Panel (2000) found that guided repeated reading procedures are effective in improving reading fluency and overall reading achievement. These procedures improve word recognition, fluency, and comprehension.

Administering Fluency Assessments

Directions. The following are some guidelines for administering fluency assessments:

- ➤ Give your daughter a reading passage she has not seen before at her instructional level.
- ➤ Fluency assessments are always done as "cold reads"; that is, they are done with material that is new to the person being tested.
- ➤ Explain that you would like her to read the passage out loud and then tell you about the story. Then say, "When you are ready, you may begin."
- ➤ Start your stopwatch when the student reads the first word.
- ➤ Follow along on your copy of the passage as the student reads. Place a line through each word that is read incorrectly or omitted.
- ➤ Place a check above each word that is read correctly.
- ➤ If your daughter substitutes or mispronounces a word, put a line through the word and write the word she said above it.
- ➤ If your daughter does not correctly say the word within 3 seconds, say the word for her and circle the word to mark it as incorrect. Self-corrections and repetitions are not marked as errors.
- ➤ At the end of one minute, stop timing and place a bracket after the last word read.

> ➢ Have your daughter finish reading the passage.
> ➢ Ask your daughter to retell the story.

How to score. Use the following steps to determine your daughter's fluency rate.

> ➢ Count the number of words read in one minute.
> ➢ Count each word you circled or put a line through. The total is the number of errors made. Subtract this number from the number of words read in one minute to arrive at the oral reading fluency rate, or words correct per minute score.
> ➢ Compare your daughter's reading rate to the scores on the Fluency Standard Table at http://www.readinga-z.com/ assess/fluency-passage.html. Fluency passages can be found at this site or purchased from http://teacher.scholastic.com/ products/fluencyformula/assessment.htm.

Scoring the retelling. Score the retelling using the following criteria. Assign an appropriate numeric score from 1 to 5 for future comparison.

> ➢ No recall or minimal recall of only a fact of two from the passage.
> ➢ Student recalls a number of unrelated facts of varied importance.
> ➢ Student recalls the main idea of the passage with a few supporting details.
> ➢ Student recalls the main idea along with supporting details, although not necessarily organized logically or sequentially as presented in the passage.
> ➢ Student recalls a comprehensive summary of the passage, presented in a logical order and/or with details, and includes a statement of the main idea.
> ➢ Student makes reasonable connections beyond the text to her own personal life, another text, or other source.

Activities to Develop Fluency

Repeated readings. The more your daughter hears or reads a story, the better she comprehends it and the more she will love it (Harvey & Goudvis, 2000). S. Jay Samuels (1979) has developed an instructional procedure to help students increase their fluency and accuracy through rereading. The steps in the individualized procedure are:

➢ Have the students choose a textbook or trade book and read a passage from the book aloud while you record the reading time and any errors.

➢ Have the student practice rereading the passage orally or silently several times. Then have the student reread the passage and record the reading time.

➢ Have the student compare her reading time between the first and last readings. Then the student prepares a graph to show her growth between the first and last readings.

Reader's theater. Reader's theater is a dramatic performance of a script by a group of readers (Black & Stave, 2007). It is a reading activity in which readers read stories or plays with expressive voices and use gestures to help the audience visualize the action (Sloyer, 1982). In reader's theater, each student assumes a part, rehearses by reading and rereading her character's lines in the script, and then does a performance of the reading for her classmates or audience. The backbone of reader's theater is repeated reading, a tested and proven method for increasing reading fluency in short-term studies (National Reading Panel, 2000). Classroom-based research has found that the reader's theater approach to fluency instruction leads to significant improvement in reading fluency and overall reading achievement (Morrow & Gambrell, 2011).

There are multiple advantages of using reader's theater with students, including:

➢ The level of difficulty of different parts within a script can vary widely (Worthy & Prater, 2002).

> ➢ Students have an opportunity to enjoy reading good literature and, by doing this, they engage with text, interpret characters, and bring the text to life (Keehn, Harmon, & Shoho, 2008).
> ➢ Reader's theater incorporates the principles of effective fluency instruction, such as modeling fluent reading, assisted reading, and repeated reading, within an authentic and purposeful framework (Morrow & Gambrell, 2011).
> ➢ Reader's theater is a highly motivating and engaging reading activity (Morrow & Gambrell, 2011).

To incorporate reader's theater in your daughter's reading instruction, begin by choosing the right text. You can choose scripts you find online, pull them from books of plays, or create your own scripts. Texts for reader's theater are chosen based on the age of the students, the length of the text, and the suitability of the language and plot. The steps for reader's theater include:

1. *Adapt the text.* To adapt a text to reader's theater, choose the selection your daughter likes as a script, eliminate the parts that are unnecessary, and highlight the characters' names. The length and complexity of the text should be appropriate for the age and reading ability of your daughter. You may want to retype the selection into a script-like format.
2. *Rehearse.* Select a text, then read and discuss it while clarifying the meaning of unfamiliar vocabulary. On the second reading, your daughter repeats each line in a choral response after you. Discuss how to use her voice, gestures, and facial expressions to interpret the character she is reading. Read the script several times, aiming for accurate pronunciation, voice, and inflections.
3. *Perform.* Reader's theater can be presented on a "stage" or in front of the family. During the performance, readers usually hold the script in their left hand, so that the right hand is free for gestures. If the reader is sitting, she may stand to read her lines. If she is standing, she may step forward to read. The emphasis should be on expressive quality of the reader's voices and intonation.

Your daughter can create her own reader's theater scripts from stories she has read about or topics that are related to thematic units learned in school (Flynn, 2004). Ask your daughter to complete a "quick write" in her journal to reflect on what she liked about her reader's theater practice and performance. As a family, you can create backgrounds, costumes, masks, or props. Creating the background and set allows a better understanding of a story's setting, purpose, and intended audience. Following the performance, talk about the experience, either as performers or as listeners.

The following are web sources for reader's theater scripts:

➤ http://www.aaronshep.com/rt/
➤ http://www.teachingheart.net/readerstheater.htm
➤ http://www.storycart.com
➤ http://www.readinglady.com
➤ http://www.ruyasonic.com
➤ http://www.margiepalatini.com
➤ http://www.fictionteachers.com/classroomtheater/theater.html
➤ http://www.readingonline.org/electronic/elec_index.asp?HREF=carrick/index.html
➤ http://bms.westport.k12.ct.us/mccormick/rt/RTHOME.htm
➤ http://www.vtaide.com/png/theatre.htm
➤ http://www.timelessteacherstuff.com

Reader's theater scripts can also be bought commercially from several sources:

➤ *Benchmark Education* (http://www.benchmarkeducation.com). This company has a variety of reader's theater scripts at different reading levels. The scripts are generally sold in packs for classroom use.
➤ *Portage and Main Press* (http://www.portageandmainpress.com). This company has at least five book collections of reader's theater scripts for students in kindergarten through grade 8.

> ➤ *Prufrock Press* (http://www.prufrock.com). This company has two books on reader's theater with scripts appropriate for students in grades 3–4 and 4–5. Written for teachers to use with their students, these are perfect if you choose to perform as a group.

> ➤ *Teacher Created Materials* (http://www.teachercreated.com). Ask for *Texts for Fluency Practice* by Rasinski and Griffith Resources. These texts are cowritten by fluency expert Timothy Rasinski for grades 1–8. As students regularly read and perform these age-appropriate texts, they improve their decoding, interpretation, and, ultimately, comprehension of the materials. A variety of genres are included in the texts: poetry and rhymes, song lyrics, reader's theater scripts, and famous speeches and quotations.

Additional commercial programs for developing reading fluency are Read Naturally (http://www.readnaturally.com) and the Marie Carbo Method (http://www.nrsi.com). Read Naturally provides a method for improving reading fluency by combining three strategies for improving fluency: teacher modeling, repeated reading, and progress monitoring. The Marie Carbo Method uses CDs that phrase the text in larger segments that give slower readers a chance to process the text. Readers listen to the discs three times and then they should be able to read the text back to the teacher independently. I have used both of these programs with success.

App for Fluency

◆ *K12 Timed Reading Practice.* K12 Timed Reading Practice lets readers in levels K–4 practice fluency by reading short, timed stories. The app allows readers to learn to focus on comprehension instead of decoding words. The app has more than 250 short stories for young readers, with a variety of fiction and nonfiction options at many different reading levels. Users can keep track of one reader's results or compile results for multiple readers. Results include the stories read, words per minute, and percent above or below average reading rates. In addition, users can get recommendations for moving up or down in reading difficulty based on their scores, or see what's next on the app's reading list.

Vocabulary

Research emphasizes that vocabulary development is a vital part of all content learning, but it is too often ignored. The link between vocabulary knowledge and comprehension is undeniable. Although reading a wide variety of material increases a student's vocabulary significantly, direct and explicit instruction in vocabulary must also occur. Parents must build word-rich environments in which to immerse their daughters and teach and model good word learning strategies. Because research shows that looking up words and writing definitions is the least effective way to increase their vocabulary, parents need to use innovative and engaging activities to be successful in enhancing their daughter's vocabulary.

High-Frequency Vocabulary

The Dolch Sight Words are a list of the 220 most frequently used words in the English language. These sight words make up 50%–70% of any general text. The Dolch list was developed by Dr. Edward Dolch in 1948 and published in his book *Problems in Reading*. Dolch compiled his sight word list based on the words most frequently used in children's reading books in the 1930s and 1940s. Dolch found that children who can identify a certain core group of words by sight could learn to read and comprehend better. Dolch's word lists are still widely used today and highly respected by both teachers and parents. These sight words were designed to be learned and mastered by the third grade. The list of Dolch words contains 220 words that have been arranged by levels of advancing difficulty from preprimer to third grade.

These 220 sight words include pronouns, adjectives, adverbs, prepositions, conjunctions, and verbs. In addition, there is a separate list of 95 Dolch nouns. Many of the Dolch Sight Words are difficult to portray with pictures or hard to sound out through phonics methods. Therefore, these words must be learned as sight words, and they must be quickly recognized in order to achieve reading fluency. Once children have learned and memorized these basic sight words, they will read more fluently and with greater comprehension.

Word lists by level and a variety of resources for teaching high-frequency words are available for free download at http://www.uniqueteachingresources.com/reading-sight-words.html. These lists can be made into flashcards or PowerPoint slides for fluency practice. They can also be converted into a checklist to record your daughter's progress as she masters each list.

You can select from the following activities to reinforce students' skills with the Dolch Sight Words.

➢ *Game boards.* Create a simple game board and place the target words on each space. Roll the dice or spin a spinner. As a child lands on the space, she says the word. Provide help as needed. Go to http://jc-schools.net/tutorials/gameboard.htm for downloadable game boards and directions to make dice and spinners. In addition, the site provides directions for making word cards using Microsoft Word and downloadable templates for word cards.

➢ *Trace a high frequency word.* Create high-frequency word game cards that use a dotted font. Let your child trace each letter. Cut out each card. Consider decorating the front of each card so you cannot see the word when playing games or mount onto an index card or colored paper. You can also make cards using glue and sand or glitter for tactile tracing.

➢ *Word booklets.* The Hubbard's Cupboard site (http://www.hubbardscupboard.org/printable_booklets.html) provides downloadable stories that provide practice with high-frequency words. They are available for printing in black and white as well as color.

Some additional sources of high-frequency word practice include the following websites:

➢ http://www.mrsperkins.com/dolch.htm

> ➢ http://www.quiz-tree.com/Sight-Words_main.html
> ➢ http://www.candohelperpage.com/sightvocab_1.html
> ➢ http://www.samsonsclassroom.com/

Apps for High-Frequency Words

◆ *Mastering Sight Words Levels 1, 2, and 3.* This app has a two step process. Step 1, Teach Sight Words in Context, asks children to use words in sentences. When your daughter sees words used in sentences rather than in isolation, she is more likely to remember them. She develops an understanding of the word's meaning. Sentence-based instruction is an extremely effective method for helping children learn sight words. Step 2, Teach Sight Words Through Repetition, provides repetition of words, key to sight word acquisition. Children do not learn new sight words by being exposed to them only once. This app is specially designed to maximize word exposure. Answers to the questions are chosen from a group of same-level sight words. When the answer choice is made, the student must decide between four sight word options. Each Mastering Sight Words app contains 95 fill-in-the-blank sentences and four possible answers for each sentence.

◆ *Sight Word Bingo.* This app uses a barnyard theme to teach sight words. There are five difficulty levels serving preschool through grade 3. This app takes on a game format, but does not have sound during gameplay.

◆ *Sight Word Snapper.* This application helps kids increase their reading speed. Your daughter will learn to recognize sight words and will no longer be dependent on just reading words letter by letter. The app contains exercises with the 500 most frequent words in English newspapers, as well as exercises with training words consisting of 1–6, 7–10, and 11–15 letters.

◆ *Sight Words 2.* This app contains professional voiceovers of words for excellent auditory learning. There are five built-in games for playful learning. Hard and easy levels of difficulty for games are provided. Great memory building is achieved with the memory game in this app.

◆ *Sight Words Flash Cards.* The flash cards in this app are divided into four categories: preschool, kindergarten, first grade, and second grade. Each grade has an accompanying Question Mode to test and enhance reading skills. By simply clicking on the flag button provided in each flashcard, you can add difficult words to the practice list for revisiting at a later time.

Comprehension

There are some requirements that have to be met before comprehension of text can occur (Block & Pressley, 2001; Pressley & Afflerbach, 1995):

➤ Good readers are active readers. They have clear goals in mind for their reading. They constantly evaluate whether the text, and their reading of it, is meeting their goals.

➤ Good readers typically look over the text before they read, noting things such as the structure of the text and text sections that might be most relevant to their reading goals. This can take the form of a picture walk through the text or a preview of chapters by older readers.

➤ As they read, good readers frequently make predictions about what is to come.

➤ They read selectively, continually making decisions about their reading—what to read carefully, what to read quickly, what not to read, what to reread, and so on.

➤ Good readers construct, revise, and question the meanings they make as they read.

➤ Good readers try to determine the meaning of unfamiliar words and concepts in the text, and they deal with inconsistencies or gaps as needed.

➤ They draw upon, compare, and integrate their prior knowledge with material in the text.

➤ They think about the authors of the text and their style, beliefs, intentions, historical milieu, and so on.

➢ They monitor their understanding of the text, making adjustments in their reading as necessary.

➢ They evaluate the text's quality and value and react to the text in a range of ways, both intellectually and emotionally.

➢ Good readers read different kinds of text differently. When reading narrative, good readers attend closely to the setting and characters. When reading expository text, these readers frequently construct and revise summaries of what they have read.

➢ For good readers, text processing occurs not only during actual reading but also during short breaks and after reading has ended.

➢ Comprehension is a consuming, continuous, and complex activity, but one that, for good readers, is both satisfying and productive.

With these requirements in mind, let me suggest a model for encouraging comprehension as you read with your daughter.

➢ Explain to your daughter that predicting is making guesses about what will come next in the text you are reading. You should make predictions often when you read. Start with the title and ask your daughter what she thinks the story will be about. Stop frequently as you read, discuss if your predictions were correct, and make new predictions.

➢ If she is having difficulty with predictions, model the process for her by making your own predictions. Simply say "I am going to make predictions while I read this book. I will start with the title." Explain what you think will happen.

➢ Engage your daughter in collaborative predictions. Suggest that from a certain section on you want her to make predictions with you. Each of you should stop and think about what might happen next and then discuss your thoughts.

➢ After much guided practice, it is time to let your daughter read silently and make predictions while she reads. Remind her to be sure to make predictions often and to check as she reads to see whether her prediction came true.

Choosing Well-Suited Texts

Careful attention to the level and demands of texts used is critical. When students are first learning a comprehension strategy, they should encounter texts that do not make heavy demands on extensive background knowledge, complex vocabulary, or unknown decoding skills.

The level of motivation your daughter brings to the text impacts whether and how she will use comprehension strategies (Dole, Brown, & Trathen, 1996; Guthrie et al., 1996). Therefore, allow the self-selection of reading material from preselected books to let her interests emerge and enhance motivation. Lists of texts by subject and level are available at http://www.scholastic.com/teachers/article/100-new-book-lists-created-teachers-teachers.

Activities for Comprehension

Three-Minute Pause. The Three-Minute Pause provides a chance for students to stop, reflect on the concepts and ideas that have just been read, make connections to prior knowledge or experience, and seek clarification. The Three-Minute Pause encompasses the following steps:

1. *Summarize key ideas thus far.* Can you retell the events thus far?
2. *Add your own thoughts.* What connections can be made? Does this remind you of anything that has happened to you?
3. *Pose clarifying questions.* Are there things that are still not clear? Are there confusing parts?

Graphic organizers. The purpose of a graphic organizer (see Figure 5) is to provide a visual structure for the way your daughter thinks about text. You probably remember the Venn diagram used to compare and contrast concepts. Your daughter compares things all of the time. Engage in oral practice comparing and contrasting clothes, movies, and TV shows. A large assortment of graphic organizers for reading comprehension is available at http://www.scholastic.com/teachers/lesson-plan/graphic-organizers-reading-comprehension. They can be downloaded and printed. Make a complete set, then place them in page protectors or have them laminated. Then you

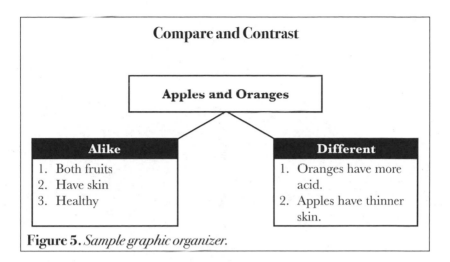

Figure 5. *Sample graphic organizer.*

can reuse them with each story you read. They can also be used with expository texts.

Questioning strategies. In 1956, Benjamin Bloom headed a group of educational psychologists who developed a classification of levels of intellectual behavior important in learning, called Bloom's taxonomy. The taxonomy has undergone revision since the original. It provides levels of cognition or thought starting with basic knowledge questions in which your daughter will define or recall specific details in the text (remember level) and goes up to the create level. Each level of Bloom's taxonomy moves up the cognitive ladder and requires greater depth of knowledge and a higher level of critical thinking (see Figure 6). Formulate questions at each level if possible. Even young girls can use higher order thinking skills. More information on Bloom's taxonomy is available at http://cft.vanderbilt.edu/teaching-guides/pedagogical/blooms-taxonomy.

Phrase-cued text lessons. Phrase-cued texts are a means to train students to recognize the natural pauses that occur between phrases in their reading. Because phrases are units that often encapsulate key ideas, the student's ability to identify them can enhance comprehension of the text (Rasinski, 1990, 1994). You will need two copies of a student passage: One annotated with phrase-cue marks and the

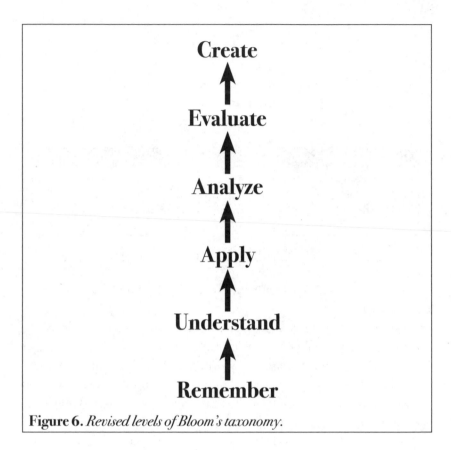

Figure 6. *Revised levels of Bloom's taxonomy.*

other left without annotation. Guidelines for preparing phrase-cued passages include the following:

> ➢ Select a passage. Select a short (100–250 word) passage that is within the student's instructional or independent reading level.

> ➢ Mark sentence boundaries. Mark the sentence boundaries of the passage with double slashes (//).

> ➢ Mark within-sentence phrase breaks. Read through the passage to locate phrase breaks—naturally occurring pause points that are found within sentences. Mark each of these phrase breaks with a single slash mark (/). Here is an example:

The Attack of the Giant Jellyfish

// Big,/ huge/ jellyfish/ that can get/ up to six feet wide/ and 450 pounds/ have drifted/ into waters/ near Japan./ This/ has set off/ some big problems/ for the fishermen/ there./ The big jellyfish/ clog/ the fishing nets./ They split/ the net/ or crush/ the other fish./ Some/ of the other fish/ die/ from the stings/ of the jellyfish./ If any fish/ make it,/ they have a lot of slime/ on them/ from the jellyfish./ This makes it hard/ to sell/ the good fish./ //

➤ Provide your daughter with the unmarked text and show her the prepared passage with phrase-cue marks inserted.

➤ Read aloud your copy of the phrase-cued text. Your daughter follows on her copy and marks her text exactly as you have. After marking each sentence, have her read the sentence back to you and then read the entire passage from the beginning to the last sentence she has marked. This incorporates repeated reading of text as well as phrasing techniques.

➤ Have your daughter read the entire passage aloud 2–3 times. Provide ongoing feedback about her reading, noting the observance of phrase breaks. Complete the session with a retelling of the story.

Apps for Comprehension Practice

◆ *Aesop's Quest.* This app, based on Aesop's fables, is a learning game where the student must remember elements of a story to complete a level. At the end of each story segment or level, the student is rewarded with puzzle pieces. After solving the puzzle, the story is complete and the child can continue to the next story. This app was developed in association with the Virginia Department of Education.

◆ *Fact or Opinion.* This is a bingo-style game that helps students practice determining if a passage is factually accurate or the writer's opinion. A correct answer allows the student to place a marker on a Bingo card. Five markers in a row wins. Levels can be played in single player mode against the computer or multiplayer against a friend.

◆ *MiniMod Reading for Details.* This app helps students practice identifying the five Ws of reading—who, what, where, when, and why. This app is carefully aligned with the new Common Core State Standards. Students can play in either practice mode or game mode. The game mode is a Bingo-like game. Students will read a passage about an inventor and his or her invention, then practice their understanding of reading for details. Each program offers three levels of reading difficulty that can be played in single player mode against the computer or multiplayer against a friend.

◆ *The Opposites.* This app helps children learn vocabulary and the corresponding antonyms by challenging them to match up pairs of opposing words in increasingly difficult levels. The game also helps children understand the importance of word context and is an opportunity for them to think about how the words they use oppose other words. The Opposites consists of 10 different levels, each stage with a corresponding level of vocabulary. The app also offers a dictionary option that provides definitions and antonyms in a kid-friendly format.

◆ *Opposite Ocean.* Characters Luna and Leo must master the magic of words by correctly identifying the antonym of each given keyword. Children earn pearls when they drag the correct bubble word to the enchanted clam. This app was developed in association with the Virginia Department of Education.

◆ *Popplet.* This is a productivity app that also works as a mind-mapping tool. Use the app to begin structuring the writing process, to create graphic organizers and classroom visuals, to organize material according to text structures (list, sequence, compare/contrast, cause/effect), and to practice sentence combining and complex sentence creation by connecting individual "popples."

◆ *Professor Garfield Fact or Opinion.* This app is part story, part game, and part online safety lesson. When Garfield's friend receives an

"F" on his report about goats for using opinions instead of facts, Professor Garfield steps in to explain the differences between a fact and an opinion (particularly with regard to the Internet), how to read with a questioning mind, and how a fact can be verified. This app was developed in association with the Virginia Department of Education.

◆ *Question Builder.* An app designed to help children learn to answer abstract questions and create responses based on inference, the use of audio clips promotes improved auditory processing for special needs children with autism spectrum disorders or sensory processing disorders. Audio clip reinforcement can be turned on or off for children without special needs.

◆ *Same Meaning Magic.* Readers help characters Luna and Leo, young magicians at magic school, toss word stones into the wishing well to earn gold coins and jewels by choosing the best synonym. This app was developed in association with the Virginia Department of Education.

◆ *Same Sound Spellbound.* An adventure designed to help the player understand homophones (words that are pronounced the same but have different meanings, such as bee and be), Luna and Leo, young magicians at magic school, must use their spellbook to bring animal statues to life. In the game, students must correctly identify the homophone that best completes the puzzle sentence within a given time. If the word is correct, the animal statue comes to life. If it's incorrect, the statue crumbles. This app was developed in association with the Virginia Department of Education.

◆ *SimpleMind.* A basic mind-mapping tool that turns your device into a brainstorming, idea-collecting, and thought-structuring device, SimpleMind's limited options make it a good tool for students who are new to mind mapping.

◆ *Speech With Milo.* This is a fun sequencing and storytelling game that asks students to slide the three picture cards into correct order (first, next, and last), then watch the story come to life. A speech-language pathologist chose Milo's activities, such as hitting a baseball or eating a sandwich, to help kids learn to organize time, sentence, and storytelling concepts with familiar themes. Several different Speech With Milo games are available, so students can stay engaged.

Assistive Technology

With knowledge of the reading process and activity suggestions, you now have the ability to work with your daughter and help her practice specific reading components. Consistency of effort is critical for you and your daughter to achieve the desired learning outcome. To become fully literate in today's world, however, students must become proficient in the new literacies of 21st-century technologies. This is especially true for dyslexic students who have limited access to traditional literacies.

Because information and communication technologies (ICTs) redefine the nature of literacy, it is incumbent on parents to explore these strategies and to integrate these new technologies into home-based literacy instruction.

As advocates for our dyslexic children, it is imperative that we embrace the myriad of possibilities technology has to offer. Our new instructional focus must take into consideration not only the child, her talents, her development, and her interests, but also technology possibilities. In addition, when exploring technology, we must explore the potential for circumventing our children's reading problems. By empowering our daughters through access to audiovisual reference libraries, they can become proficient in gathering the information that formerly was limited to textual format. As dyslexic students master the use of optical character recognition systems, they immediately gain independent access to multiple texts from which higher order thinking skills can be taught. Speech synthesizing technologies enable students to write into text the language they construct. These two technologies are but a sampling of the possibilities for circumventing reading and writing problems. Repeated access to these technologies will help develop writing and reading skills (Poplin, 1995).

Raskind and Higgins (1999) suggested several types of assistive technologies that allow persons with dyslexia to compensate for their disabilities rather than attempt to remediate them. These include word processing programs, spellcheckers, proofreading programs, outlining programs, abbreviation expanders, speech recognition, speech synthesis, optical character recognition systems, personal data managers, listening aids, talking calculators, digital reference books, and other interactive media and television.

Assistive technology is any device, piece of equipment, or system that helps bypass, work around, or compensate for an individual's specific learning challenges. Many more options exist today to help students and adults with learning differences make the most of their abilities. Assistive technology is not a cure for dyslexia, but it does provide alternative strategies for students to compensate for areas of weakness and capitalize on their strongest talents. For example, a student who struggles with reading but who has good listening skills might benefit from listening to audiobooks.

Assistive technology should be used in conjunction with remedial efforts and not as a replacement for remediation. As you explore assistive technology for your daughter you should focus on your daughter's specific needs when reviewing and considering any technology.

Some assistive technology tools I suggest include:

➢ *Audible.com* (http://www.audible.com). This is an Amazon.com-driven audiobook source. A huge catalog of titles provides multiple genres, including a wide range of children's literature. In addition to audiobooks, Audible.com is home to magazines, radio shows, podcasts, stand-up comedy, and speeches from modern culture, politics, and the business world. Monthly membership plans start at $7.49 after a 2-week free trial.

➢ *Bookshare* (http://www.bookshare.org). Bookshare is the world's largest online library of accessible reading materials, including books, textbooks, newspapers, and magazines, for people who have difficulties reading printed text. It allows members to find accessible titles and download them onto their personal computers. No limits are placed on the number of titles accessed at one time. Bookshare also gives users the option to read books in a browser with a screen reader or to listen to them on an mp3 player. Bookshare is free for all U.S. students with qualifying disabilities, thanks to an award from the U.S. Department of Education Office of Special Education Programs (OSEP).

➤ *Echo Smartpen from Livescribe* (http://www.livescribe.com/ en-us). Students can record everything they hear, say, and write, while linking their audio recordings to their notes. Once note-taking is completed, the student can quickly replay audio from the Livescribe paper, a computer, or a mobile device by tapping on their handwritten notes. The smartpen saves notes and recordings to a computer. This enables your daughter to search for words within notes.

➤ *Kurzweil 3000* (http://www.kurzweiledu.com/products.html). Kurzweil 3000 is a very useful comprehensive reading, writing, and learning software solution for any struggling reader, including individuals with dyslexia. The technology includes a talking word processor that reads text by word, phrase, or sentence. The speed can be controlled to meet the needs of your daughter. Included in the program are translation support, a dictionary option, highlighting and notetaking tools, and a talking spellchecker. However, be warned that this software is pricey—about $1,400 at the time of this book's writing.

➤ *Learning Ally* (formerly known as Recording for the Blind and Dyslexic, http://www.learningally.org). Learning Ally offers free individual membership for eligible people with visual impairments or dyslexia who experience difficulty in reading print material. Learning Ally's collection of more than 75,000 digitally recorded textbooks and literature titles are downloadable and accessible on mainstream as well as specialized assistive technology devices. To use Learning Ally, membership is required. Check out the website for specific information regarding membership requirements.

➤ *LibriVox* (http://librivox.org). LibriVox provides free audiobooks from the public domain. LibriVox volunteers record chapters of books in the public domain and release the audio files back onto the net. Their goal is to make all public domain books available as free audiobooks. Be aware that that you are limited to books published before 1923. Luckily, there is a great deal of fantastic literature from which to choose.

➢ *NaturalReader10* (http://www.naturalreaders.com/index.php). NaturalReader10 is easy-to-use software that can read to your daughter any text from virtually any location. This includes texts contained in Microsoft Word files, webpages, PDF files, and e-mails. In addition, NaturalReader can also convert any written text into audio files such as MP3 or WAV using natural sounding voices. A free downloadable version is available on the website. Expanded versions are available starting at $49.50.

➢ *The Readingpen 2 and Readingpen TS by Wizcom Technologies* (http://www.wizcomtech.com/eng/home/a/01/lang/index. asp). This is a great portable learning tool for students with reading difficulties. Using the pen, the reader develops a feeling of autonomy and fluency which enhances text comprehension. Users can scan and insert text using the touch screen and virtual keyboard, hear it spoken aloud, obtain definitions, and correct pronunciation within seconds. All looked-up words can be transferred to the PC for further practice. Text can also be uploaded from the PC onto this fully mobile, lightweight pen, where it can be read aloud.

➢ *Project Gutenberg* (http://www.gutenberg.org). This is a volunteer effort to digitize and archive cultural works, to "encourage the creation and distribution of eBooks." Founded in 1971 by Michael S. Hart, it is the oldest digital library. You may choose among free epub books or free Kindle books, and download them or read them online. The service is free but donations are accepted.

Assistive Technology Apps

◆ *Audiobooks.* This app contains more than 5,000 classic audiobooks, plus a growing collection of newer titles. A paid version is also available to eliminate ads.

◆ *Audiobooks for Your Kids.* This app contains 30 classic children's books.

◆ *Dragon Dictation.* This voice recognition application allows you to easily speak and instantly see your text or e-mail messages. You may need an external microphone for some devices.

◆ *Dragon Go!* This is an accurate way to search online content using your voice. Search queries from a variety of top websites, including Google, Yahoo, YouTube, Twitter, and Wikipedia.

◆ *Free Audiobooks.* This app includes best-selling and professionally narrated audiobooks; new premium titles are added monthly.

◆ *Image to Speech.* This application allows you to take a picture and the application will read out loud the text inside the image.

◆ *Jagamaga Audiobooks.* This app includes more than 200 titles, plus hundreds of free short fiction pieces; the fiction is searchable by genre, title, author, and narrator. If your daughter needs to read classic literature for a class, find it on your Jagamaga app and listen to it anytime on your phone. You can listen and follow along with your book and make notes.

◆ *MindNode.* A simple-to-use mind-mapping application that helps to visually collect, classify, and structure ideas and organize, study, and solve problems. Mind maps can be used for many different tasks—including to-do lists, brainstorming, holiday planning, research, writing, project management—and in many different environments including school and home.

◆ *Pocket (Formerly Read It Later).* This is a simple text-to-speech program worth exploring as no Internet connection is needed to use it.

◆ *QuickVoice Recorder.* This app provides one-touch recording for memos, e-mail, dictation, lists, meetings, classes, or entire lectures.

◆ *Say It and Mail It.* This app allows users to record an e-mail, then send it. Some devices may require an external microphone to use.

◆ *Talk Mail Lite.* This app allows users to listen to their e-mails out loud. Two months of the app are free, then you can upgrade to the Talk Mail Pro version for a fee. The app reads aloud e-mails received via Google, MobileMe, or AOL Mail; basically, any IMAP-enabled e-mail account. For Microsoft Exchange or Yahoo, users can sync their e-mail account with MobileMe or use auto-forwarding.

◆ *Typ-O.* Typ-O uses a powerful word prediction engine and sophisticated spelling error model to help users write, even if their spelling isn't perfect.

◆ *vBookz.* This is a book reader with voices that are really quite fantastic. vBookz has worked to expand upon Apple's iBooks, keeping much of the design and functionality used by iBooks while adding a text-to-speech feature.

◆ *VoiceOver and Voice Control.* Apple devices come equipped with the VoiceOver feature that serves as a screen reader for those with visual disabilities. By touching or scrolling your finger across the screen, you will be told exactly what lies beneath your fingertips. When you wish to write an e-mail or send a text message, VoiceOver will echo every letter you select and then speak it again to confirm it. With Voice Control for Android, you can easily call or play music by speaking the name of the person or artist you would like to hear.

◆ *Web Reader!* Web Reader! uses text-to-speech technology along with web page content recognition to read web pages to users. The user can configure web pages to be read as soon as they are loaded, read pages manually after they are loaded, or use cut and paste to read only sections of text.

◆ *ZenTap.* This a word prediction system that allows you to complete words simply by typing the first letters. It features auto completion, spell check, a wider typing screen, and the possibility to change the font size. For those who struggle with the iPhone keyboard, this may be a good option.

The Future

In the era of new literacies and new technologies, West (1991) proposed that those who are now called dyslexic may be in a position of privilege in the upcoming world. The new market for ability and skills may increasingly devalue the conventional literate accomplishments that have carried such high prestige for hundreds of years. This new market may gradually begin to reward the creative, visual-thinking dyslexics who have had such a difficult time in a traditionally literate society. It is possible that these individuals may be recognized for the talents and strengths they have always exhibited rather than being penalized or excluded. In the new era of literacy, their weaknesses will come to be seen as increasingly inconsequential.

This post-literate society will require new schools to adjust their focus to emphasize the ability to quickly access and correctly assess the implications of pertinent information, regardless of its source. Working memory limitations will be circumvented because access to information will take precedence over committing information to memory. As such trends continue, perhaps a shift in policy focus will occur. Instead of focusing on obsolete standardized test scores, teachers will be able to attend to ensuring equitable learning conditions for all children in every school and in every classroom.

Conclusion

As we have gone forward on our journey, you have learned more about the reading process and what you can do to help your daughter succeed. The time you spend with your daughter is invaluable but it is not sufficient. A struggling reader needs the support and expertise of a reading specialist trained to provide the help your daughter so desperately needs. You may have to step into the role of legal advocate to make sure this happens, as further explained in Chapter 7.

CHAPTER 7

Becoming Your Daughter's Advocate

You are on a journey, a crusade, a quest. Your goal is simple—to ensure that your daughter receives every possible legal, administrative, and educational assistance she needs in order to achieve success in the reading process. However, the achievement of this goal is difficult and requires a significant commitment and hard work on your part.

In pursuit of your quest, you are going to have to use every persuasive tool available with regard to your interactions with the school system. You are going to have to know more and be better prepared than the school is. You are going to have to be better organized, clearer, more concise, and focused on your outcomes. You are going to have to be cunning and just plain outwork others. Your controlling mantra must reflect Winston Churchill's famous words, "Never, never, never, never give up" until you are successful.

Rev. Martin Luther King, Jr. said, "Rarely do we find men who willingly engage in hard solid thinking. There is an almost universal quest for easy answers and half-baked solutions. Nothing pains some people more than having to think." These words are applicable here.

There are no easy answers or quick solutions. Is this process difficult? Yes. Does it take a great deal of commitment and hard work? Yes. But, is it worth it to help your daughter be successful? Yes! Don't get lost in the weeds. Don't get distracted or chase false rabbit trails. Keep your eyes on the prize. Your quest is to make your daughter's life richer by helping her in the reading process. All that is important is that your daughter succeeds.

How All of This Works for You—Success Formula

As you prepare to interact with the school system in the pursuit of your quest, you must focus on the outcome of ensuring that your daughter receives all of the appropriate educational assistance she needs. To accomplish this, it is necessary for you to understand some basic facts. First, the relationship between you and the school system is potentially antithetical and adversarial by its very nature. It is absolutely essential for you to have this perspective and understanding. The school system's agenda may be quite different than yours. The opposite may also be true—you may be lucky enough to be in a school district that works quite hard to meet the needs of its students with special needs. Just know that this isn't always the case. Keep this in the back of your mind as you begin your efforts to garner the school's assistance in meeting your child's special needs.

For the most part, the school system is a giant, administrative morass. The goal of this monolith is inertia and the status quo. It is awash in rules, regulations, and policies, many of which bear no relevance to your daughter's needs. The system's every action is driven by the desire to avoid change, save money, and preserve the status quo. Schools are built upon broad, generic applications of educational services that are geared to address generic kids and produce generic outcomes. They have a "one program fits all" mentality, and they want to apply this "one program" to your daughter. Schools want to spend as little time, money, or effort as possible. Even the many good, sympathetic local school personnel tend to be stifled and controlled in this process. The school system provides no incentive or patience for them to come up with creative, individualized approaches and solutions for your child's individual needs. The school's rules, policies, and regulations must be followed and your daughter's needs are often secondary.

Conversely, you are focused on your daughter as an individual. You are attempting to overthrow the generic status quo. You are seeking personalized services that will address your daughter's individualized needs. You are not concerned about money or effort. You just want whatever modifications or changes that may be necessary to help your daughter. You are focused on and driven by your daughter's success.

The two positions could not be more opposite. However, recognizing, accepting, and merging these two divergent perspectives is absolutely critical to the success of your quest. To be successful, it is necessary for you to be smarter, nicer, better prepared, more stubborn, more tenacious, and more committed to addressing your daughter's needs.

Secondly, it is absolutely necessary for you to be pleasant and professional in all of your dealings with the school system. Think about the old saying, "You catch more flies with honey than with vinegar." By this point, you have probably had a long history with the school system— a long history of frustration and stunted success. Much water has passed under the bridge. Yet, you must remember that these are the very people you need to help your daughter with the special services and accommodations she will receive once your efforts are successful. You do not want to "win the battle, but lose the war." Your quest is not about trying to "win," to make yourself feel good, or to belittle the other side. It is not about you. It is about ensuring that your daughter receives the assistance necessary for her success.

You need to put your emotions aside. Use them, but harness them in a positive way to help energize you as you move through this difficult process. It does not help to yell or call people names. Many of the people you will be face-to-face with are teachers or administrators who may well agree with you, but who are not able to officially offer support because of the school system's rules, policies, and procedures. They likely care about your daughter, but they also have to comply with the system. They do not have complete flexibility, but you want to be sure they remain predisposed to assist your daughter once you are successful.

Again, this rule is without exception—remain pleasant and professional at all times. Remember, you will succeed. You just want to be sure you bring the good, caring teachers and administrators along with you. You want to be sure your daughter receives the services she needs and deserves.

Knowledge, Clarity, and Persistence

As you step into the shoes of advocate, the road becomes a little foggy. There are times you may be uncertain as to exactly what you want for your daughter. Other times you may have slightly paranoid thoughts that there is a hidden agenda behind the many meetings you attend. You'll see friendly faces and some that are unknown. You will want to trust the smiling faces, but something tells you to be wary. This process is a combination of extreme preparedness and intuition. To make this all work, the responsibility falls heavily on your shoulders. The three elements that are your guiding principles are knowledge, clarity, and persistence. You must immerse yourself in knowing the law and procedural guidelines. You must have clarity relative to your daughter's needs. You must be dogged in your persistence to obtain each and every service your daughter needs to become a competent reader. It will not be easy but the payoff is huge. So let's get started.

Knowledge

Never forget that knowledge is power. That is particularly true when you are attempting to cajole the school system into providing necessary services for your daughter. As I mentioned, you have to be smarter, harder working, more committed, and better prepared. But most of all, you have to be more knowledgeable about your daughter's needs and what rights and resources are available, as well as how your daughter qualifies for receipt of those resources.

Know your daughter. You must know your daughter. Certainly you know and love your daughter. You know how much she needs, deserves, and wants to succeed. But you must compile a complete factual record of your daughter's personal and educational profile that can be used as compelling factual support for the services you are seeking. You need to compile every document you have received from or sent to the school system or school personnel about your daughter. This includes all of the letters, teachers' notes, memos, e-mails, evaluations, reports, correspondence, or written documentation of any kind received from or sent to the school system. Also you need all reports, evaluations, and recommendations acquired from any private professionals you might have retained.

As part of this process, you have a right to request that the school system provide you with a copy of your child's file or files, including, but not limited to, all tests, reports, assessments, protocols, grades, notes by teachers or other staff members, memos, photographs, correspondence, e-mails, and so forth. In short, you need a copy of everything in your daughter's school files. Also, you should request copies of related and relevant documents prepared by or sent to any private professionals retained or consulted by the school system.

Next, you must be sure you understand that there is no such thing as informal communications with the school system or its personnel. All communications should be formal and in writing. For example, if you run into a teacher in the hall and have a verbal conversation relevant to your daughter, you should always follow up with something in writing that at a minimum repeats and confirms the relevant portions of the verbal discussions. You should also request a written confirmation from the other party.

Once you have compiled all of these documents, you need to develop a complete understanding and working knowledge of their content. You need to know, understand, and be able to refer to what each and every person has said about your daughter. You will likely need to retain a psychologist, educational advocate, or other professional in order to assist you with the development of a complete interpretation and understanding of technical terms, phrases, and educational jargon used in evaluations or reports related to your daughter.

You are now ready to compile all of the documents into a file. This file must be all inclusive. It must be organized and indexed in a manner that makes any document immediately locatable. The file needs to be easily transportable, and you should take it to every formal meeting you have with school personnel. You will be amazed how many times you will be in such a meeting and the school personnel will either not have knowledge or have incorrect knowledge of the content of some crucial document or report. You response should be to immediately locate the relevant documents and correct any inaccuracies.

Know the law. You need to know the applicable law. In this process, it is important to recognize that a law has two parts. The first is the substantive content of the law that describes and defines how it is applicable and what type of relief or support it provides. Secondly, laws also have a procedural component that defines the steps, requirements, and time limitation with which you must comply in order to be eligible to receive the substantive benefits under the law. You must first ensure that you comply with the procedural aspects of the law and ensure you are qualified to receive its benefits before you can even consider evaluating the benefits.

It is absolutely necessary that you read and reread the law. You must develop a working knowledge and command of the law that is applicable to the services you are seeking for your daughter. You must know what the law says and specifically how your daughter qualifies under the law for the specific services you are seeking. The applicable "law" includes federal statutes, federal regulations, commentary statements in the Federal Register, and state laws, as well as administrative rules, policies, and procedures of the school system or even the local school. You must understand and address all of these.

In the last portion of this chapter, you are provided with a brief summary overview of three federal statutes that could assist you in your quest to help your daughter. These include the Individuals with Disabilities Education Improvement Act (2004), which provides that all children with qualifying disabilities receive a free appropriate public education designed to meet their special education needs. Also included in this chapter is a brief overview of the No Child Left Behind Act (2001). This statute provides that all children, including children with learning disabilities, have an opportunity to obtain quality, research-based reading assistance. It includes a diagnostic/assessment framework to ensure that students reach appropriate grade-level competency in a timely manner. Lastly, there is an overview of Section 504 of the Rehabilitation Act of 1973. This is a civil rights law and not a special education law. Its purpose is to use reasonable modifications or adaptations to protect disabled persons from discrimination. This includes reasonable program or procedural modifications necessary to ensure that children with learning disabilities receive an appropriate education. Although very limited in both depth and breadth, the summaries of these statutes will provide you with an introduction into some of the relevant aspects of the law.

Gaining an understanding of the law and school rules or policies is not easy—it requires time and effort—but it can and must be done. In the end, you must understand the law so that you know what benefits are or are not available to your daughter, as well as what it takes for her to be eligible to receive them. In short, the law must be known thoroughly and complied with completely in order to be used effectively on your child's behalf.

However, it is just as important for you to know and understand the law in order to be able to rebut any inaccurate positions taken by the school system. The school system can misinterpret or misapply the law. School personnel may not fully understand it. They may not know or accurately understand or apply the facts of your daughter's case to the law. When such inaccuracies happen, it is incumbent on you to step up and point out the appropriate corrections. Your file documentation on your daughter will allow you to correct any factual misunderstanding. However, your superior knowledge of the law and its proper application will give you a clear advantage in the process of persuasion.

It is necessary for you to know, use, apply, and explain your position using the applicable law's specific terminology. Accurate use of terminology is crucial to accurate outcomes. An example of this can arise if you refer your daughter for a private evaluation. You will need to ensure that the evaluator has a complete working understanding of the language of the law. For example, if the evaluator's report identifies the "best" educational services for your child, then the report will not be applicable to the school system's final consideration. This is because, according to the law, your child is only entitled to an "appropriate education," not the "best education." The language must be accurate.

You can obtain assistance in your efforts to understand the law from numerous sources. There are many local parent support groups and organizations. There are educational advocates, legal advocates, countless articles, and websites that provide a plethora of information and explanation, including:

> *Electronic Code of Federal Regulations* (http://www.ecfr.gov). This site provides the full text of various statutes and regulations, as well as text and Boolean search capabilities within the text.

> *Families and Advocates Partnership for Education* (http://www.fape. org/contact.htm). This organization provides information and training on IDEA and related topics at workshops, brown bag seminars, satellite video conferences, and online training. The site includes referrals to national, state, and local disability organizations and advocates and to a nationwide network of parent training and information centers and community parent resource centers. Information on research about best practices that can be used to improve educational services is also available.

> *National Center for Learning Disabilities* (http://www.ncld.org). This site connects parents to important resources, articles, links, and guides for LD, dyslexia, and special education services. It also offers a "Parents Guide to Dyslexia," identifies educational rights and opportunities, and shares topical videos, articles, and links.

> *Parent to Parent USA* (http://www.p2pusa.org). Administered through local and state organizations, this group provides emotional and informational support to families of children who have special needs, most notably by matching parents seeking support with an experienced, trained "Support Parent." The site provides training, reference resources, and referrals.

> ➢ *Wrights Law Special Education Law and Advocacy* (http://www.
> wrightslaw.com). This is an excellent resource on all topics
> related to special education. It includes topical information,
> legal libraries incorporating a vast array of resources on legal
> issues, cases, and regulations, and commentaries regarding
> applicable laws. Multiple website links on all relevant topics,
> plus a newsletter, DVDs, books, and live seminars are offered.

Know school system personnel. You need to know the school
system personnel who will be making the decisions regarding the
special services you are seeking for your daughter. You are entitled
to notice of any scheduled meetings, including an identification of
who will attend. Review the attendance list carefully. It is important
for you to know who you are meeting with and what his or her orientation is with regard to such issues. Look through the attendance
list and immediately identify the persons you know. You need to prepare a brief written dossier on each. Know who might be receptive
of your position and helpful to your quest. Although his or her ability
to publically support you may be limited, such support behind closed
doors could be crucial. Find out how the individuals on your child's
team have decided in previous cases and the specific concerns that
they have raised that you will need to address. But remember, if the
services you seek will greatly increase the workload of an individual or
cause him to be in disfavor with his bosses for bucking the status quo,
he may be less than excited about your requests. As for any persons
you do not know, find out about them. Learn their positions and their
prior responses to the type of issues you are raising. Talk to parents
who have been through the process of seeking similar services for their
child. They may be able to provide real insight as to the orientation
of your child's team members. Lastly, write down the information you
gain and review it before each meeting.

Clarity

In the movie *Cool Hand Luke*, the old prison warden kept telling Paul
Newman's inmate character (who continually challenged the prison's

rules), "What we've got here is failure to communicate." Unfortunately, most fights, arguments, divorces, and even wars arise from a failure of two sides to effectively communicate. In this process with the school system, it is absolutely essential that you have done all of the difficult work of learning the law and learning your daughter's complete history. However, once all of the hard work is done, it is of no value unless you can communicate clearly and concisely to the school system what you want for your daughter and why she is entitled to it.

Be prepared to provide input during your daughter's IEP meeting. Your time to present at your child's case meeting will be short and the other members' attention span will be even shorter. You need to distill your entire claim—facts and law—into a 5-minute "elevator speech." Your orientation and identification must be short, clear, concise, and accurate as to the law and facts. Further, you are only going to get what you ask for, so be sure to specifically identify the assistance you are seeking. Your statement should include:

➢ your daughter's specific needs;
➢ the factual basis and identification of the documents that support the needs you identify;
➢ the specific portions of each law that identify what accommodations or services to which your daughter is entitled;
➢ the specific reasons why the school system's profile of your daughter and interpretation of the law are inaccurate; and
➢ specifically what assistance, services, or accommodations you are seeking for your daughter.

Attending meetings. It is vitally important that you attend each and every meeting. The school system personnel must give you timely notice of every meeting, and they have an obligation to make every effort to ensure that the meetings are held at a time and place that are convenient for you.

It is critical for you to attend each and every meeting and actively inject yourself into the discussions and decisions. If you are not present, the process will move on without you, and decisions will be made with which you might not agree. You will have no chance to control the outcomes. However, if you attend the meetings, and if you have followed all of the ideas we have addressed and done all of your home-work, then you will be the person at the meeting who can provide the most accurate and complete history of your daughter, as well as the most accurate interpretation of the law. You will have the knowledge. You will have the power. You be able to control and direct favorable outcomes from the meeting. In essence, you will control the moment.

Personal journal. You should keep a private comprehensive journal that chronicles each and every aspect of your quest. This should include meetings, findings, recommendations, outcomes, and personnel involved. It is for your use only. However, it will allow you to have a quick, comprehensive review of all that has previously trans-pired. From meeting to meeting, participating school personnel may change and not know the complete prior history, they might misstate the prior occurrences, or they may have forgotten. By reviewing your journal before each meeting, you will be able to maintain and convey a consistent, accurate account of what has been accomplished to date. You will not have to back up and redo what has already been done. Again, knowledge is power and by having such information you will make yourself the indispensable participant in the process.

Taping meetings. Buy a small, pocket-size digital recorder. You are not trying to be secretive. Before each meeting begins, you should openly state that you intend to record it. Put the recorder right out on the table.

This action is important for a couple of reasons. First, it is intimi-dating and will require the school system personnel to be careful and measured as to what they say and do. Secondly, it will also allow you the opportunity to have a complete, accurate record of what was said and decided upon. You will then need to have these recordings tran-scribed so that you have an accessible record of the proceedings. Many school systems record meetings themselves. On their assurance that you can receive a copy of the recording, you might be willing to forgo your taping efforts. However, such a waiver of your rights is not rec-ommended. You need to maintain control over the information. This is the only way you can ensure that the information is retained, accu-rately transcribed, and available in a timely manner to you.

Notes. Even though you are taping the proceedings, you want to take notes during the meeting of issues that have special importance. Specifically, you want to be sure to write down any stated findings or recommendations. Before the meeting ends, read your notes to the group, and be sure your reading is included in the minutes. Then, make sure you have a confirmation of their accuracy on the record before the meeting adjourns.

Minutes. Before the close of the meeting, you should request a copy of the minutes and a copy of the outcomes of the meeting. When received, the formal minutes need to be verified against your taped transcription. This is the best way to ensure the completeness and accuracy of the school system's records.

Persistence

I cannot stress the need to be an advocate more than this: This is about your daughter. This is about your daughter's future. This is about your daughter's life. This is about ensuring that your daughter receives the support and services necessary to guarantee her success. It is vital and the most important thing you can do. It is necessary for you to ensure that your daughter receives all of the assistance to which she is entitled.

As previously indicated, you must maintain a professional attitude. You must be nice in every way, but you must make "nice noise." You must make more noise than anyone else. You must be aware of everything that is going on with your child every day. You must continually ask questions and raise issues. Whenever school system personnel look at your daughter, they should know that their every action or nonaction will be reviewed. They should feel a positive level of discomfort. They should feel the accountability of having someone looking over their shoulder every day. You need to be the nicest person in the world who will be there every day, asking the hard questions, fighting the status quo, and working continuously and tirelessly for your daughter.

You will encounter significant pushback as you work to challenge the status quo and assert your daughter's rights. But you must not be deterred. Don't be embarrassed or intimidated. Don't accept no as an answer. If you have done your homework effectively, then you will know more about your daughter's needs and your daughter's rights under the law than anyone in the school system. You will intimidate them. The message is to hang in there with the professionals   be bold. The quest is for your daughter. Work it every day. Know what you are entitled to and what you want. Go for the whole enchilada. Do not settle for anything less. Your daughter deserves it. If you are not successful at one level, appeal to the next. Don't stop—don't lose your focus—and never give up.

The Law

The remaining portions of this chapter provide a very limited overview of several federal laws that are potentially applicable to your quest. Neither the laws nor the summaries are in any way intended to be all-inclusive.

The primary emphasis addresses the Individuals with Disabilities Education Improvement Act (IDEA; 2004). This is the primary statute for special education and related services for children with identified learning disabilities. However, also included in this chapter are very limited overviews of the No Child Left Behind Act (NCLB; 2001) and Section 504 of the Rehabilitation Act of 1973. Although these statues have a broad reach, they can work in conjunction with IDEA to offer educational standards, processes, and procedures, as well as supportive services, for qualifying disabled children. However, do not forget that there exists a plethora of federal and state laws, as well as local policies, procedures, and guidelines that also address issues that support children's educational services.

This material can seem technical and dry. It is not necessarily an "easy read." However, your quest is not an easy journey. To be successful, you must read, understand, evaluate, and develop a complete working knowledge of the primary sources of this information. A difficult task? Yes! But it is a task that is absolutely necessary to ensure your daughter's success.

Overview of Individuals With Disabilities Education Improvement Act of 2004

Special education law for children with disabilities finds its roots in 1975 with the passage of the Education for All Handicapped Children Act. Since that time, the law has been amended and changed several times, with the most recent iteration being the Individuals with Disabilities Education Improvement Act (2004), or IDEA. Congress identified the purpose of IDEA as ensuring that all children with disabilities have available to them a free appropriate public education (FAPE) that emphasizes their unique needs and prepares them for further education, employment, and independent living. In addition, IDEA ensures that the rights of children with disabilities and parents of such children are protected. The primary funding mechanism for IDEA comes from federal grants to the states. While assisting the states in the provision of special education and related services, IDEA also allows the respective states control over the application of many aspects of the special education process.

Special education services provided under IDEA require specifically designed instructional goals and procedures intended to meet the unique needs of eligible disabled children. Further, these services are to be provided at no cost to the parents. IDEA also includes a comprehensive system of procedural safeguards designed to engage parents and ensure their participation in the educational decisions made for their disabled child. Further, IDEA provides parents with the availability of a comprehensive administrative and judicial due process review of any decisions with which they disagree. IDEA has four main parts:

> ➤ Parts A and B cover eligibility procedures, regulations, and required educational services for disabled children between the ages of 3 through 21.
> ➤ Part C pertains to services for infants and toddlers with disabilities under the age of 3.
> ➤ Part D discusses national activities that have been promoted to enhance educational services for children with disabilities.

Your focus as a parent seeking services under IDEA will be on Parts A and B. Under these portions of IDEA, a free appropriate public education is made available to all qualifying disabled children between the ages of 3 and 21. To be eligible, a child must be identified as having a disability as defined under IDEA, including a specific learning disability such as dyslexia. Eligible children receive special education and related services under an Individualized Education Program (IEP). The IEP identifies a child's educational status, the specific nature of any disability, and individualized services, as well as annual, academic, and functional goals and measures used to track a child's progress.

Special Education Services

IDEA lists 13 specific categories of disabilities that are covered and that qualify a child to receive special education services. Aside from these specifically identified categories of qualifying disabilities, a child is eligible for special education and related services under IDEA if she has a specific learning disability. A specific learning disability is defined as a disorder of one or more of the basic psychological processes involved in understanding or using spoken or written language. According to IDEA, this specifically includes dyslexia.

Evaluations to determine your daughter's needs. Before initiating special education and related services under IDEA for a child suspected of having a disability that interferes with her ability to learn, the local educational agency (LEA) must conduct a full, comprehensive, and individualized evaluation of the child. The request for an initial evaluation can be initiated by either the parents or the LEA. An LEA proposing to conduct such an evaluation must provide proper notice to the parents. The notice must fully describe why the evaluation is to be conducted, the nature and extent of any proposed evaluation procedures, as well as an identification of each action that is being proposed.

Aside from providing notice, the LEA must also obtain informed parental consent, or at least make every reasonable effort to obtain an informed consent, before it proceeds with such an evaluation. If the parents fail to respond to such a request or refuse to provide consent for the evaluation process, then the requesting LEA may attempt to obtain parental consent through procedural safeguards under IDEA.

The initial evaluation should consist of evaluative tools necessary to determine whether or not the child has a qualifying disability, as well as the child's educational needs in light of such a disability. Upon the completion of the assessments and other evaluative measures, the parents and a group of qualified professionals on the evaluation team determine whether the child has a qualifying disability under IDEA, as well as the educational needs of the child. In the compilation and interpretation of the evaluation information, the LEA is required to draw upon a variety of sources, including aptitude and achievement tests, parental input, and teacher recommendations. If it is determined that the child has a disability and is entitled to special education and related services under IDEA, then an IEP must be developed for the child. A copy of the evaluation report and the documentation of the potential eligibility determination must be provided to the child's parents.

The compilation and evaluation of this broad spectrum of information will help to ensure that the child's IEP reflects accurate information regarding the child's current educational status, her needs, the specific nature of any disability, and individualized services to be provided to the child. Such a complete assessment picture of the child will assist in the identification and development of annual academic and functional goals and measures used to identify the child's progress toward goal attainment.

What Happens When Your Daughter Qualifies for Special Education and Related Services Under IDEA

The determination that a child qualifies for special education services under IDEA must be made by the child's parents and a "team of qualified professionals." The team must include the child's "regular teacher" or a classroom teacher qualified to teach children the same age as the child. Also included should be at least one person qualified to conduct individual diagnostic evaluations such as a school psychologist, speech-language pathologist, or remedial reading teacher.

This determination is based upon the existence of a qualifying specific learning disability. The decision is supported by all evaluative data collected, including research-based interventions. Data can include, but is not limited to, documentation that shares:

> - that the child has a specific learning disability;
> - the basis for making the determination;
> - the relevant behavior noted during the observation of the child and the relationship of the behavior to academic functioning;
> - any educationally relevant medical findings;
> - that the child does not exhibit age-appropriate achievement or meet, or make sufficient progress toward, state-approved grade-level standards or intellectual development;
> - if the child participated in the Response to Intervention (RtI) process that assessed the child's response to scientific, research-based intervention;
> - the instructional strategies used, the student-centered data collected, and the child's response to the scientific research-based intervention provided as part of the child's participation in the RtI process;
> - that the child's parents were notified about the state's policies regarding the amount and nature of student performance data that would be provided;
> - educational services that would be provided;
> - strategies for increasing the child's rate of learning; and
> - the parents' right to request an evaluation.

Individualized education programs. Once a child's qualifying disability is properly identified, IDEA requires that an Individualized Education Program (IEP) be developed. An IEP team is responsible for the creation and implementation of the child's IEP. This team includes the parents, special education and regular teachers, and a representative of the LEA, as well as an individual who can interpret the instructional implications of any evaluation results.

In developing a child's IEP, the team must consider the strengths of the child, the concerns of the parents, the results of the initial or most recent evaluation, as well as the academic, developmental, and functional needs of the child (IDEA, 2004). Also, if necessary, the team must consider the appropriateness of any positive behavioral interventions, supports, and strategies to address any behavioral issue that potentially interferes with the child's success under the IEP.

The IEP document is a child's individualized "game plan" or "road map" for services under IDEA. IDEA is very specific as to what information must be included in an IEP. The requirements include, but are not limited to, an identification of the child's present level of academic achievement and functional performance, a statement of measurable annual academic and functional goals, a description of benchmarks or short-term objectives, and a statement of any appropriate individual accommodations.

The LEA is also charged with conducting periodic reviews of a child's IEP in order to evaluate the achievement of progress toward the identified goals, as well as any needed amendments. Such a review should be conducted no less than annually. The IEP should be revised as necessary to address any lack of progress toward these goals and any additions or modifications that need to be made in order to enable the child to attain the identified goals (IDEA, 2004).

Make no mistake about it, if your daughter is determined to be eligible for special education services under IDEA, an accurate and appropriate IEP is absolutely required for her ultimate success. Therefore, it is critical for you to go to the law to learn and understand what IDEA requires to be included in an IEP. Then, as a parent and member of the IEP team, you must insert yourself into the process. You must ensure the sufficiency of the IEP's content, its accuracy as it relates to your daughter's history, and its concordance with the law. Do not approve or sign-off on the document until all of your concerns have been addressed.

Procedural Safeguards

Parental participation. Parents of a disabled child are required members of any group empowered to make decisions regarding the special educational services or related placement of their child. IDEA mandates that prior notice be provided to the parents of the purpose, time, and location of any meetings. The notice must also include the identification and professional credentials of the persons who will attend. If neither parent can personally attend a scheduled meeting, the LEA must attempt to use other methods in order to facilitate their participation. This can include conference calls, Skyping, or video conferencing. If, despite all documented efforts, the local agency is unable to obtain the parents' participation, then the group may move forward with its decisions.

Independent educational evaluations. If the parents of a child with a qualifying disability under IDEA (2004) disagree with the evaluation obtained by the LEA, they have the right to request an independent educational evaluation of their child at public expense. If the LEA does not approve the free independent evaluation requested by the parents, the parents always have the right to obtain an evaluation at their own expense. If the parents obtain such an independent educational evaluation at public expense or share with the LEA an evaluation obtained at private expense, the results of the evaluation must be considered in any decisions related to the provision of special education and related services to the child.

Parental notice. The LEA must provide the parents of a child with a disability with reasonable, timely, written notice if the LEA either proposes to initiate changes or refuses to initiate changes in the identification, evaluation, or educational placement of the child. IDEA is very specific as to the nature and content of the information or explanations contained in such a notice.

Procedural safeguards notice. A notice of procedural safeguards under IDEA is a written notice of a child's rights and procedural remedies available under the law. IDEA requires that a copy of this notice be given to the parents of a qualifying disabled child at least once a school year. However, additional copies must also be provided to the parents upon the initial referral of a child, upon the parents' request for an evaluation, upon the filing of a due process complaint, or at the request of the parents.

It is absolutely critical that you are aware of all the rights and remedies available to your daughter under IDEA. You must obtain a copy of this document every year.

Mediation. The LEA must ensure that procedures are in place to allow disputes to be resolved through a mediation process. The mediation process must be voluntary on the part of both parties, not used to deny or delay any party's rights, and be conducted by a qualified mediator. The state must bear the cost of any mediation process. If the parties successfully resolve their dispute through the mediation process, then they must execute a legally binding settlement agreement. Although the agreement is admissible and binding in any subsequent court action, the actual discussions during the mediation process remain totally confidential and may not be subsequently divulged.

Filing a due process complaint. The parents of a disabled child or the LEA may file a "due process complaint" that addresses any alleged violation of IDEA as it relates to the identification, evaluation, or educational placement of their child or the provision of an appropriate education. In general, such alleged violations are limited to those that occurred not more than 2 years before the complaining party knew or should have known that they occurred.

IDEA identifies very specific information that must be included in such a complaint. The applicable state department of education is required to develop and make available to parents model forms to assist in the drafting and filing of a due process complaint. However, use of these forms is not required. All that is required is that the due process complaint as filed must comply with the stated requirements identified in IDEA.

There are a number of time limitations and specific procedural requirements related to both the filing of a due process complaint, the response to the complaint, and additional related resolution processes. If you intend to file such a complaint, then you need to carefully review the applicable section of IDEA and ensure that you are in full compliance with all substantive and procedural requirements.

Impartial due process hearing. If the issues identified in a due process complaint cannot be informally resolved by the parties, then a due process hearing is conducted by an impartial hearing officer. This is a formal hearing on the issues identified in the due process complaint. It is governed by the specific rules of administrative procedures (Logsdon, n.d.). The hearing process involves the production of documentary evidence, witness testimony, and the cross-examination of witnesses. Subject to the dictates of the applicable formal administrative procedures, each party has the right to be accompanied by legal counsel or persons with knowledge and training with regard to children with disabilities.

It should be noted that a legal advocate may provide invaluable assistance to you at this stage of the proceedings. As indicated, it is a formal hearing process based upon established administrative procedures. The LEA will likely be represented by its legal counsel. Thus, the litigation experience of such an advocate could be beneficial. Further, if the party's dispute has gone this far without resolution, the introduction of a legal advocate would likely do little to aggravate the already severely heightened adversarial relationship.

Hearing decision and appeals. The parents are entitled to a copy of any decision by the hearing officer. Any such decision is subject to possible appeal by either party. The appeal process includes, if allowed under applicable state law, an appeal to the applicable state board of education. However, once all applicable administrative appeals have been exhausted, either party may appeal the hearing officer's decision to the applicable federal court.

Disciplinary Issues

Parents of children with learning disabilities know all too well that their child's learning frustrations can manifest themselves as behavioral issues. IDEA provides protections and limitations with regard to the nature and extent of disciplinary actions the LEA may apply to a disabled child. In general, school personnel may remove a child with a disability who violates a code of student conduct to an appropriate interim alternative educational setting or another setting, or suspend the child for not more than 10 consecutive school days (to the same extent applicable to nondisabled children). Any additional removals of not more than 10 consecutive days in the same school year for separate incidents of misconduct are allowed subject to limitations. IDEA requires that after a child with a disability has been removed from her current placement for 10 days, any subsequent removals during the same school year require the LEA to provide services that enable the child to continue to participate in the general curriculum and continue progress toward the IEP goals. Also, the child must receive a functional behavioral assessment (FBA), behavioral intervention services, and modifications designed to address the behavior involved so that it does not reoccur.

Within 10 days of any decision to change the placement of a child with a disability because of a violation of a code of student conduct, the local agency, the parents, and the relevant members of the IEP team must determine if the conduct in question was caused by, or had a direct and substantial relationship to, the child's disability, or if it was a direct result of the LEA's failure to implement the child's IEP. If a determination is made that the behavior in question was a direct result of the LEA's failure to implement the child's IEP, then immediate steps must be taken to remedy those deficiencies. If the decision is made that the behavior in question was a manifestation of the child's disability, then the IEP team must conduct a functional behavioral assessment (FBA) and see that it is implemented. If a behavioral assessment has already been conducted, then it is to be reviewed and modified as appropriate.

IDEA also contains an identification of special circumstances behaviors that include things such as possession of weapons or illegal drugs and serious bodily injury to another at school, on school property, or at a school function. Such an occurrence would allow for the removal of the disabled child to an alternate setting for not more than 45 days. This can be accomplished without regard to whether or not the behavior is determined to be a manifestation of the child's disability.

On the date that the decision is made to make a change of placement of a child with a disability because of a violation of the student code of conduct, the LEA must notify the parents. The parents are also entitled to a procedural safeguards notice as identified in IDEA. These safeguards also allow the parents a right to appeal any disciplinary placement. A disabled child who qualifies for special education services under IDEA remains entitled to these services even if she is expelled from school for disciplinary reasons.

Child Placed in a Private School or Facility

When a child with a disability is placed by the state or LEA in a private school or facility as a means of carrying out its obligations to provide appropriate special education and related services required under IDEA, the law requires such a placement to be accomplished at no cost to the child. Such a child has all of the rights under IDEA that a child would have had if the services had been provided by the LEA.

If the LEA makes a free appropriate public education available to a disabled child, then it is not necessarily required to pay the cost for providing special education and related services to the child if the parents voluntarily choose to place the child in a private school. However, IDEA provides the parents the right to appeal any denial by the LEA.

No Child Left Behind Act of 2001 and Section 504 of the Rehabilitation Act of 1973

The primary focus in this chapter has been on IDEA. However, there are other legislative sources of educational support for children with learning disabilities. It is important to recognize and understand how each complements or interfaces with IDEA in order to provide educational assistance to children with learning disabilities, including reading problems. These various laws include, but are not limited to, the No Child Left Behind Act (NCLB; 2001) and Section 504 of the Rehabilitation Act of 1973. Although not written specifically for children with disabilities, NCLB provides for scientifically based reading instruction and evaluation directed toward the assurance that all children reach appropriate grade-level performance in a timely manner, as well as support services for children who need additional assistance to reach these goals.

Section 504 prohibits discrimination against persons with disabilities when those disabilities interfere with life functions, including learning. Identified disabilities can include learning disabilities. Section

504 provides for the provision of significant accommodations in the learning process to assist disabled children. The following outline of relevant portions of these two acts helps to identify how these laws relate to, interface with, or support IDEA and children with learning disabilities.

No Child Left Behind Act of 2001

NCLB (2001) is a reauthorization of the Elementary and Secondary Education Act (1965). It provides federal money to public schools to be used toward achievement of accountability-based educational achievement goals (Education Week, 2011). NCLB has to be reauthorized every 5 years. However, the original authorization expired in 2007 and Congress has been funding NCLB through extensions ever since. Sweeping changes have been proposed to NCLB and, at this time, a number of states have been granted waivers that allow for a delay/modification of a number of the NCLB requirements (Rothstein, 2009).

NCLB supports standards-based educational reform centered on the premise that setting high standards and measurable goals can improve individual outcomes in education. NCLB requires states to develop assessments in basic skills and to assess all students at selected grade levels in order to receive the applicable federal school funds. NCLB does not assert a national achievement standard. However, NCLB expanded the federal role in public education through annual testing, annual academic progress, report cards, teacher qualifications, and funding changes (Education Week, 2011).

With regard to its support for the reading process, NCLB differs from IDEA and Section 504 in that a child is not required to have a formal diagnosis of a disability in order to receive benefits under the law. However, children who struggle with reading tend to fall behind their nondisabled peers most and profit the most from NCLB's assistance (Marshall, 2004).

The purpose of NCLB (2001) is to ensure that all children have a fair, equal, and significant opportunity to obtain a quality education and reach, at a minimum, proficiency as determined by academic standards and academic assessment tools. To accomplish this stated purpose, NCLB puts a high priority on promoting reading achievement and requires that schools establish reading programs that are founded upon scientifically based reading research. This is research that relies on scientific measurements and observational methods of collecting data. The stated goal is to ensure that every student can read at grade level or above not later than the end of grade 3 (Margolin & Buchler, 2004). NCLB defines reading as a complex system of deriving meaning from print that includes:

➤ the skills and knowledge to understand how phonemes, or speech sounds, are connected to print;

➤ the ability to decode unfamiliar words;

➤ the ability to read fluently;

➤ sufficient background information and vocabulary to foster reading comprehension;

➤ the development of appropriate active strategies to construct meaning from print; and

➤ the development and maintenance of a motivation to read.

NCLB requires that reading programs must provide explicit and systematic instruction in the areas of phonemic awareness, phonics, vocabulary development, reading fluency (including oral reading skills), and reading comprehension strategies. The improvement process under these reading programs is achieved through the application of scientifically based reading research. This process:

➤ applies rigorous, systematic, and objective procedures to obtain valid knowledge relevant to reading development, reading instruction, and reading difficulties;

➤ includes research that employs systematic, empirical methods that draw on observation or experiment;

➤ involves rigorous data analysis that are adequate to test the stated hypotheses and justify the general conclusions drawn;

➤ relies on measurements or observation methods that provide valid data across evaluators and observers and across multiple measurements and observations; and

> ➢ have been accepted by a peer-reviewed journal or approved by a panel of independent experts through a comparably rigorous, objective, and scientific review. (NCLB, 2001, 20 U.S.C. 6368(6))

NCLB creates time-relevant achievement goals for your child's development of reading proficiency. Specifically, it requires that all children read on grade level no later than the end of the third grade. NCLB identifies the essential components of reading instruction. It also requires that reading programs use scientifically based reading research in order to provide explicit and systematic instruction in the areas of phonemic awareness, phonics, vocabulary development, reading fluency (including oral reading skills), and reading comprehension strategies. NCLB offers supplemental services often given by private providers, including some programs geared specifically to students with dyslexia (Marshall, 2004).

NCLB is certain to undergo significant changes and modifications in the next few years. However, at this time, the majority of the proposed modifications (and the multiple waivers that have been issued to multiple states) have been directed primarily toward the accountability/measurability/sanctions arising from the achievement/accountability portions of the law. The instructional portions of NCLB have been subjected to fewer changes. Thus, at this time (and until changed), it is important to recognize that NCLB provides potentially significant reading assistance to your child. Unless it is changed, NCLB puts a high priority on promoting reading achievement (Marshall, 2004).

Section 504 of the Rehabilitation Act of 1973

Section 504 of the Rehabilitation Act of 1973 is not a special education law. It is a civil rights law that is intended to prevent discrimination against persons with a disability by institutions receiving or benefiting from public funds. It defines an individual with a disability as a person who has a physical or mental impairment that limits one or more major life activity. The protected major life activities include, but are not limited to, "learning" and are applicable to "specific learning disabilities." As a general rule, if a child is eligible for services under IDEA (2004), she qualifies for protection under Section 504. However, not all students covered under Section 504 are eligible for IDEA services. Section 504 has a much broader definition of disabilities and so it applies to more people (National Center for Learning Disabilities, 2006).

Section 504 provides that no individual or student with a disability shall be discriminated against because of that disability. The law provides that all disabled students are entitled to a free appropriate public education. Such a free appropriate public education requires the provision of regular or special education aids and services designed to adequately meet the educational needs of students with disabilities to the same extent the needs of nondisabled students are met.

Parents seeking to have their child receive appropriate educational support with regard to a learning disability should submit a written notice to the LEA requesting an evaluation to determine if the child has a disability under Section 504 that presents a significant impact on the child's ability to learn. This request should be submitted to the LEA's Section 504 Coordinator and the principal (who usually serves as the coordinator). You should include in your request copies of any evaluations or medical documentation you have that support your request. This request document should be hand delivered or at a minimum sent via registered mail. In addition to parental initiation of such requests, a referral can come from anyone, including a school nurse, teachers, counselor, or any professional familiar with the child's accommodation needs. In fact, the child can even make a self-referral request.

It is important to recognize that the procedures related to the handling of a Section 504 request are local in nature. Therefore, you should obtain a copy of your school district's policies and procedures related to Section 504. These documents will help inform you of your rights and the school's rights and responsibilities in the provision of the necessary accommodations (National Center for Learning Disabilities, 2006).

Evaluation reviews under Section 504 must draw from a variety of sources (National Center for Learning Disabilities, 2006). Ultimately, a group decision is made by persons with knowledge of the child, applicable evaluation data, and consideration of available reasonable educational accommodations (National Center for Learning Disabilities, 2006). The LEA is required to develop a reasonable plan to accommodate the child's disability and remove any barriers that might prevent the disabled student from participating fully in the programs and services provided through the general curriculum. This plan does not have to be in writing. Although an IEP is not required under Section 504, if the child is also eligible under IDEA, then in most cases, the IEP will be an inclusive substitute for the Section 504 plan. Although the final plan does not require parental consent, the LEA is required to provide notice to the parents of the plan decided upon (Council for Exceptional Children, 2002).

The LEA is required to develop a reasonable plan to accommodate the child's disability and remove any barriers that might prevent the disabled child from fully participating in the general curriculum. Some examples of the kinds of reasonable modifications or adaptations that might be provided under Section 504 for children with learning disabilities include things such as (Council For Exceptional Children, 2002):

> ➢ *Presentation.* Provide audio tapes, large print, oral instructions, repeat directions
> ➢ *Response.* Allow verbal responses, a scribe to record response, response via computer, tape recorder
> ➢ *Timing/Scheduling.* Allow frequent breaks, extend time allotments
> ➢ *Setting.* Provide special seating, small group setting, private room
> ➢ *Equipment and material.* Provide calculator, amplification equipment, manipulatives

Local educational agencies must also provide for impartial hearings for parents who disagree with their child's identification, evaluation, or placement. Although parents must have an opportunity to participate and be represented by counsel if they choose, under Section

504 the hearing's procedural details and parents' rights are left to the discretion of the LEA (Council for Exceptional Children, 2002).

The LEA must also provide for impartial hearings for parents who disagree with their child's identification, evaluation, or placement. Although parents must have an opportunity to participate and be represented by legal counsel if they choose, under Section 504, the hearing's procedural details and parents' rights are left to the discretion of the local education agency (Council for Exceptional Children, 2002).

Conclusion

The journey you will take as your daughter's advocate and teacher is one of empowerment. You can never leave your daughter's academic future fully in the hands of the educators. Many educators are taught from their first day on the job to never suggest any services outside the purview of the general education classroom. The school may even be counting on your ignorance of the process so as to delay the paperwork-laden process of providing any type of special services for your daughter. This is motivated by a decline in educational budgets and the additional costs required to hire specialized personnel.

The stakes are too high to be shy. The stakes are too high to delay. Just ask Lucy, Susie, Molly, and Sharon about the impact that waiting can have on the lives of your daughters. It is my hope that the urgency of taking action has been driven home. Please visit me at http://www.whycantmydaughterread.com. And never, never, never give up on your daughter.

References

Alexander-Passe, N. (2004). *A living nightmare: An investigation of how dyslexics cope at school.* Paper presented at the Sixth British Dyslexia Association International Conference. Retrieved from http://www.bdainternationalconference.org/2004/presentations/mon_s6_d_12.shtml

Alexander-Passe, N. (2008). The sources and manifestations of stress amongst school-aged dyslexics, compared with sibling controls. *Dyslexia, 14,* 291–313.

Allington, R. L. (2001). *What really matters for struggling readers: Designing research-based programs.* New York, NY: Addison Wesley Longman.

Allington, R. L., & Cunningham, P. (1996). *Schools that work.* New York, NY: HarperCollins College.

Alvermann, D. E. (2001a). *Effective literacy instruction for adolescents.* Chicago, IL: National Reading Conference.

Alvermann, D. E. (2001b). Reading adolescents' reading identities: Looking back to see ahead. *Journal of Adolescent & Adult Literacy, 44,* 676–690.

American Association of University Women. (1992). *How schools short-change girls: The AAUW report: A study of major findings on girls and education.* New York, NY: Marlow.

185

Applebee, A., Langer, J., Nystrand, M., & Gamoran, A. (2003). Discussion-based approaches to developing understanding: Classroom instruction and student performance in middle and high school English. *American Educational Research Journal, 40,* 685–730.

Armstrong, T. (1987). *In their own way: Discovering and encouraging your child's personal learning style.* Los Angeles, CA: Jeremy Tarcher.

Ash, G. E. (2002, March). Teaching readers who struggle: A pragmatic middle school framework. *Reading Online, 5*(7). Retrieved from http://readingonline.org/articles/art_index.asp?HREF=ash/index.html

Ash, G. E., Kuhn, M. R., & Walpole, S. (2009). Analyzing "inconsistencies" in practice: Teachers' continued use of round robin reading. *Reading and Writing Quarterly, 25,* 87–103.

Au, K. H., & Kawakami, A. J. (1985). Research currents: Talk story and learning to read. *Language Arts, 62,* 406–411.

Badian, N. A. (2005). Does a visual-orthographic deficit contribute to reading disability? *Annals of Dyslexia, 55,* 28–52.

Bakhtin, M. M. (1981). *The dialogic imagination.* Austin: University of Texas Press.

Bandura, A. (1997). *Self-efficacy: The exercise of control.* New York, NY: W. H. Freeman.

Banks, J., Cochran-Smith, M., Moll, L., Richert, A., Zeichner, K., LePage, P., . . . McDonald, M. (2005). Teaching diverse learners. In L. Darling-Hammond & J. Bransford (Eds.), *Preparing teachers for a changing world: What teachers should learn and be able to do* (pp. 232–274). San Francisco, CA: Jossey-Bass.

Bettie, J. (2003). *Women without class: Girls, race and identity.* Berkeley: University of California Press.

Black, A., & Stave, B. (2007). *Comprehensive guide to readers theatre.* Newark, DE: International Reading Association.

Blachman, B. A., Ball, E. W., Black, R., & Tangle, D. M. (2000). *Road to the code: A phonological awareness program for young children.* Baltimore, MD: Brookes.

Block, C. C., & Pressley, M. (2001). *Comprehension instruction: Research-based best practices.* New York, NY: Guilford.

Boaler, J., & Greeno, J. G. (2000). Identity, agency and knowing in mathematics worlds. In J. Boaler (Ed.), *Multiple perspectives on mathematics teaching and learning* (pp. 171–200). Stanford, CA: Elsevier Science.

Bos, C., Mather, N., Dickson, S., Podhajski, B., & Chard, D. (2001). Perceptions and knowledge of preservice and inservice educators about early reading instruction.

Annals of Dyslexia, 51, 98–120.

Bourdicu, P. (1986). The forms of capital. In J. G. Richardson (Ed.), *Handbook of theory and research for the sociology of education* (pp. 241–258). New York, NY: Greenwood Press.

Bourdieu, P., & Passeron, J. C. (1990). *Reproduction in education, society and culture*. London, England: Sage.

Broughton, M. A., & Fairbanks, C. M. (2002). Stances and dances: The negotiation of subjectivities in a reading/language arts classroom. *Language Arts, 79*, 288–296.

Brozo, W. G. (2000). Hiding out in secondary classrooms: Coping strategies. In D. W. Moore, D. E. Alvermann, & K. A. Hinchman (Eds.), *Struggling adolescent readers: A collection of teaching strategies* (pp. 51–56). Newark, DE: International Reading Association.

Cazden, C. (1986). Classroom discourse. In M. Wittrock (Ed.), *Handbook of research on teaching* (pp. 432–463). New York, NY: Macmillan.

Chall, J. (1983). *Stages of reading development*. New York, NY: McGraw Hill.

Cochran-Smith, M. (1984). *The making of a reader*. Norwood, NJ: Ablex.

Cohen, E. G. (1972). Sociology and the classroom: Setting the conditions for teacher-student interaction. *Review of Educational Research, 42*, 441–452.

Coleman, J. C. (1988). Social capital in the creation of human capital. *American Journal of Sociology, 94*, 95–120.

Compton-Lilly, C. (2007). The complexities of reading capital in two Puerto Rican families. *Reading Research Quarterly, 42*, 72–98.

Council for Exceptional Children. (2002). *Understanding the differences between IDEA and Section 504*. Retrieved from http://www.ldonline.org/article/6086

Davidson, R., & Snow, C. (1995). The linguistic environment of early readers. *Journal of Research in Childhood Education, 10,* 5–21.

Davies, B. (2003). *Shards of glass: Children reading and writing beyond gendered identities.* Cresshill, NJ: Hampton Press.

de Graaff, S., Verhoeven, A., Bosman, M., & Hasselman, F. (2007). Integrated pictorial mnemonics and stimulus fading: Teaching kindergartners letter sounds. *British Journal of Educational Psychology, 77,* 519–539.

DeJordy, R. (2008). Just passing through: Stigma and identity decoupling in the work place. *Group and Organization Management, 33,* 504.

Dole, J. A., Brown, K. J., & Trathen, W. (1996). The effects of strategy instruction on the comprehension performance of at-risk students. *Reading Research Quarterly, 31,* 62–88.

Dyslexia Association of Singapore. (2009). *About dyslexia.* Retrieved from http://www.das.org.sg/about-dyslexia/

Dyson, A. H. (1995). Writing children: Reinventing the development of childhood literacy. *Written Communication, 12,* 4–46.

Edelsky, C., Altweger, B., & Flores, B. (1991). *Whole language: What's the difference?* Portsmouth, NH: Heinemann.

Education for All Handicapped Children Act of 1975, Pub. Law 94–142 (November 29, 1975).

Education Week. (2011). *No child left behind.* Retrieved from http://www.edweek.org/ew/issues/no-child-left-behind

Ehri, L. C., & McCormick, S. (2004). Phases of word learning: implications for instruction with delayed and disabled readers. In R. B. Ruddell & N. J. Unrau (Eds.), *Theoretical models and processes of reading* (5th ed.). Newark, DE: International Reading Association.

Elementary and Secondary Education Act of 1965, §142, 20 U.S.C. 863.

Elliott, J. G., & Gibbs, S. (2008). Does dyslexia exist? *Journal of Philosophy of Education, 42,* 475–491.

Englert, C. S., & Palincsar, A. S. (1991). Reconsidering instructional research in literacy from a sociocultural perspective. *Learning Disabilities Research and Practice, 6,* 225–229.

Field, J. (2003). *Social capital.* London, England: Routledge.

Finders, M. J. (1997). *Just girls: Hidden literacies and life in junior high*. New York, NY: Teachers College Press.

Flynn, R. (2004). Curriculum-based readers theatre: Setting the stage for reading and retention. *The Reading Teacher, 58*, 360–365.

Freire, P. (1970). *Pedagogy of the oppressed*. New York, NY: Herder and Herder.

Frith, U. (1999). Paradoxes in the definition of dyslexia. *Dyslexia, 5*, 192–214.

Gaffney, J., & Anderson, R. C. (2000). Trends in reading research in the United States: Changing intellectual currents over thirty years. In M. L. Kamil, P. B. Mosenthal, P. D. Pearson, & R. Barr (Eds.), *Handbook of reading research* (Vol. III, pp. 53–74). New York, NY: Lawrence Erlbaum.

Gaub, M., & Carlson, C. (1997). Gender differences in ADHD: A meta-analysis and critical review. *Journal of the American Academy of Child and Adolescent Psychiatry, 8*, 1036–1045.

Gee, J. P. (1996). *Social linguistics and literacies: Ideology in discourses* (2nd ed.). London, England: The Falmer Press.

Gilger, J. W., Pennington, B. F., & DeFries, J. C. (1991). Risk for reading disabilities as a function of parental history in three samples of families. *Reading and Writing, 3*, 205–217.

Gilligan, C. (1982). *In a different voice: Psychological theory and women's development*. Cambridge, MA: Harvard University Press.

Goffman, E. (1959). *The presentation of self in everyday life*. New York, NY: Anchor Books.

Goodman, K. S. (1967). Reading: A psycholinguistic guessing game. *Journal of the Reading Specialist, 6*, 126–135.

Goodman, K. S. (1993). *Phonics phacts*. Portsmouth, NH: Heinemann.

Goodman, K. S. (1996). *Ken Goodman on reading*. Portsmouth, NH: Heinemann.

Gough, P. R., Alford, J. A., & Holley-Wilcox, P. (1981). Words and contexts. In O. J. Tzeng & H. Singer (Eds.), *Perception of print: Reading research in experimental psychology* (pp. 85–90). Hillsdale, NJ: Erlbaum.

Grant, L., & Rothenberg, J. (1986). The social enhancement of ability differences: Teacher-student interactions in first- and second-grade reading groups. *The Elementary School Journal, 87*, 29–49.

Griffiths, V. (1995). *Adolescent girls and their friends: A feminist ethnography.* Beatty, NV: Avebury Books.

Guthrie, J. T., & Davis, M. H. (2003). Motivating struggling readers in middle school through an engagement model of classroom practice. *Reading and Writing Quarterly, 19,* 59–85.

Guthrie, J. T., Van Meter, P., McCann, A. D., Wigfield, A., Bennett, L., Punndstone, C. C., . . . & Mitchell, A. M. (1996). Growth of literacy engagement: Changes in motivations and strategies during concept-oriented reading instruction. *Reading Research Quarterly, 31,* 306–332.

Hall, S. (2009). *Early signs of a reading difficulty.* Retrieved from http://www.greatschools.net/LD/identifying/early-signs-of-reading-difficulty.gs?content=739

Hallgren, B. (1950). Specific dyslexia: A clinical and genetic study. *Acta Psychiatrica Scandinavica, 65,* 179–189.

Harvey, S., & Goudvis, A. (2000). *Strategies that work.* York, MA: Stenhouse.

Hiebert, E. H. (1983). An examination of ability grouping for reading instruction. *Reading Research Quarterly, 18,* 231–255.

Hinshelwood, J. (1917). *Congenital word blindness.* London, England: H. K. Lewis & Co.

Ho, C. S. H., Chan, D. W. O., Leung, P. W. L., Lee, S. H., & Sang, S. M. (2005). Reading-related cognitive deficits in developmental dyslexia, attention-deficit/hyperactivity disorder, and developmental coordination disorder among Chinese children. *Reading Research Quarterly, 40,* 318–337.

Holland, D., Lachicotte, W., Skinner, D., & Cain, C. (1998). *Identity and agency in cultural worlds.* Cambridge, MA: Harvard University Press.

Hull, G., & Schultz, K. (2001). Literacy and learning out of school: A review of theory and research. *Review of Educational Research, 71,* 575–611.

Individuals with Disabilities Education Improvement Act, Pub. Law 108-446 (December 3, 2004).

International Dyslexia Association. (2002). *Frequently asked questions about dyslexia.* Retrieved from http://www.interdys.org/FAQ.htm

Juel, C., & Minden-Cupp, C. (2004). Learning to read words: Linguistic units and instructional strategies. In R. B. Ruddell & N. J. Unrau (Eds.), *Theoretical models and processes of reading* (5th ed.). Newark, DE: International Reading Association.

Just, M. A., & Carpenter, P. A. (1980). A theory of reading: From eye fixations to comprehension. *Psychological Review, 87,* 329–354.

Kaufman, L. N., & Hook, P. E. (1996). *The dyslexia puzzle: Putting the pieces together.* Newton, MA: International Dyslexia Society, New England Branch.

Keehn, S., Harmon, J., & Shoho, A. (2008). A study of readers theater in eighth grade: Issues of fluency, comprehension, and vocabulary. *Reading & Writing Quarterly, 24,* 335–362.

Kutz, E. (1997). *Language and literacy: Studying discourse in communities and classrooms.* Portsmouth, NH: Boyton/Cook Publishers.

Lardieri, L., Blacher, J., & Swanson, H. (2000). Sibling relationships and parent stress in families with children with and without learning disabilities. *Learning Disability Quarterly, 23,* 105–116.

Lave, J., & Wenger, E. (1998). *Communities of practice: Learning, meaning, and identity.* Cambridge, England: Cambridge University Press.

Leigh, A. H. (2006). Anything but lazy: New understandings about struggling readers, teaching, and text. *Reading Research Quarterly, 11,* 424–444.

Lieberman, P. (1992). On the evolution of human language. In J. A. Hawkins & M. Gell-Mann (Eds.), *The evolution of human languages* (pp. 21–47). New York, NY: Perseus Publishing.

Lin, A. (2008). *Problematizing identity: Everyday struggles in language, culture, and education.* New York, NY: Lawrence Erlbaum.

Logsdon, A. (n.d.). *Special education due process hearing.* Retrieved from http://learningdisabilities.about.com/od/disabilitylaws/a/due_process_hea.htm

Lyon, G. R. (1999). In celebration of science in the study of reading development, reading difficulties, and reading instruction: The NICHD perspective. *Issues in Education: Contributions from Educational Psychology, 5,* 85–115.

Margolin, J., & Buchler, B. (2004). *Critical issue: Using scientifically based research to guide educational decisions.* Retrieved from http://www.ncrel.org/sdrs/areas/issues/envrnmnt/go/go900.htm

Marshall, A. (2004). *No child left behind.* Retrieved from http://www.netplaces.com/parenting-kids-with-dyslexia/additional-legal-protections/no-child-left-behind.htm

Mayes, S., & Calhoun, S. (2000). Prevalence and degree of attention and learning problems in AD/HD and LD. *The AD/HD Report, 8*(2), 14–16.

Mayo Clinic. (2012). *Preparing for your appointment.* Retrieved from http://www.mayoclinic.com/health/dyslexia/DS00224/DSECTION=preparing-for-your-appointment

McCarthey, S. (2001). Identity construction in elementary readers and writers. *Reading Research Quarterly, 36,* 122–151.

McDermott, R., & Varenne, H. (1995). Culture as disability. *Anthropology & Education Quarterly, 26,* 324–348.

Minuchin, P. (1988). Relationships within the family: A systems perspective on development. In R. A. Hinde & J. Stevenson-Hinde (Eds.), *Relationships within families: Mutual influences* (pp. 7–26). New York, NY: Oxford University Press.

Moats, L. C. (1994). The missing foundation in teacher education: Knowledge of the structure of spoken and written language. *Annals of Dyslexia, 44,* 81–102.

Moje, E. B., & Dillon, D. R. (2006). Adolescent identities as demanded by science classroom discourse communities. In D. E. Alvermann, K. A. Hinchman, D. W. Moore, S. F. Phelps, & D. R. Waff (Eds.), *Reconceptualizing the literacies in adolescents' lives* (pp. 85–106). Mahwah, NJ: Lawrence Erlbaum.

Moje, E. B., & Luke, A. (2009). Literacy and identity: A review of perspectives on identity and their impact on literacy studies. *Reading Research Quarterly, 44,* 415–437.

Moje, E. B., Young, J. P., Readence, J. E., & Moore, D. W. (2000). Reinventing adolescent literacy for new times: Perennial and millennial issues. *Journal of Adolescent & Adult Literacy, 43,* 400–410.

Moll, L., Amanti, C., Neff, D., & Gonzalez, N. (2001). Funds of knowledge for teaching: Using a qualitative approach to connect homes and classrooms. *Theory Into Practice, 31,* 132–141.

Morgan, E., & Klein, C. (2001). *The dyslexic adult in a non-dyslexic world.* London, England: Whurr.

Morrow, L., & Gambrell, L. (2011). *Best practices in literacy instruction.* Urbana, IL: National Council of Teachers of English.

National Center for Learning Disabilities. (2006). *Accommodations for students with LD.* Retrieved from http://www.ldonline.org/article/Accommodations_for_Students_with_LD

National Center for Learning Disabilities. (2012). *What is dyslexia?* Retrieved from http://www.ncld.org/types-learning-disabilities/dyslexia/what-is-dyslexia

National Institute of Child Health and Human Development. (2000). *Report of the National Reading Panel. Teaching children to read: An evidence-based assessment of the scientific research literature on reading and its implications for reading instruction* (NIH Publication No. 00–4769). Washington, DC: U.S. Government Printing Office

National Reading Panel. (2000). *Teaching children to read: An evidence based assessment of the scientific research literature on reading and its implications for reading instruction: Reports of the subgroups.* Bethesda, MD: National Institute of Child Health and Human Development.

No Child Left Behind Act, 20 U.S.C. §6301 (2001).

Nöthen, M., Schulte-Körne, G., Grimm, T., Cichon, S., Vogt, I., Müller-Myhsok, B., . . . Remschmidt, H. (1999). Genetic linkage analysis with dyslexia: Evidence for linkage of spelling disability to chromosome 15. *European Child & Adolescent Psychiatry, 8,* 50–56.

O'Connor, M. C., & Michaels, S. (1993). Aligning academic task and participation status through revoicing: Analysis of a classroom discourse strategy. *Anthropology and Education Quarterly, 24,* 318–335.

Orenstein, P. (1994). *Schoolgirls: Young women, self-esteem, and the confidence gap.* New York, NY: Knopf.

Orton, S. (1919). Word-blindness in school children. *Archives of Neurology and Psychiatry, 14,* 285–516.

Osman, B. (1997). *Learning disabilities and ADHD: A family guide to living and learning together.* New York, NY: Wiley & Sons.

Palincsar, A. S., & Brown, A. L. (1984). Reciprocal teaching of comprehension-fostering and comprehension-monitoring activities. *Cognition and Instruction, 2,* 117–175.

Paulson, E. J. (2005). Viewing eye movements during reading through the lens of chaos theory: How reading is like the weather. *Reading Research Quarterly, 3,* 338–358.

Pennington, B. F., & Lefly, D. L. (2001). Early reading development in children at family risk for dyslexia. *Child Development, 72,* 816–833.

Pipher, M. (2005). *Reviving Ophelia: Saving the selves of adolescent girls.* New York, NY: Ballantine.

Polacco, P. (1998). *Thank you, Mr. Falker.* New York, NY: Scholastic.

Pollard, A., & Filer, A. (1999). *The social world of pupil career. Strategic biographies through primary school.* London, England: Cassell.

Poplin, M. (1995). The dialectic nature of technology and holism: The use of technology for the liberation of the learning disabled. *Learning Disability Quarterly, 18,* 131–140.

Pressley, M. (2002). *Reading instruction that works: The case for balanced teaching* (2nd ed.). New York, NY: Guilford.

Pressley, M., & Afflerbach, P. (1995). *Verbal protocols of reading: The nature of constructively responsive reading.* Hillsdale, NJ: Erlbaum

Rasinski, T. V. (1990). *The effects of cued phrase boundaries on reading performance: A review.* Kent, OH: Kent State University.

Rasinski, T. V. (1994). Developing syntactic sensitivity in reading through phrase-cued texts. *Intervention in School and Clinic, 29,* 165–168.

Raskind, M., & Higgins, E. (1999). Speaking to read: The effects of speech recognition technology on the reading and spelling performance of children with learning disabilities. *Annals of Dyslexia, 49,* 251–281.

Rothstein, R. (2009). *The prospects for No Child Left Behind.* Retrieved from http://www.epi.org/publication/pm149

Sadker, M., & Sadker, D. (1994). *Failing at fairness: How our schools cheat girls.* New York, NY: Touchstone.

Samuels, S. J. (1979). The method of repeated readings. *The Reading Teacher, 32,* 403–408.

Section 504 of the Rehabilitation Act, 29 U.S.C. Section 706 et. Seq. (1973).

Shaywitz, S. E. (2003). *Overcoming dyslexia: A new and complete science-based program for reading problems at any level.* New York, NY: Vintage.

Silverman, L. (2002). *Upside-down brilliance: The visual spatial learner.* New York, NY: Touchstone.

Sloyer, S. (1982). *Readers' theater: Story dramatization in the classroom.* Urbana, IL: National Council of Teachers of English.

Smith, F. (1982). *Understanding reading: A psycholinguistic analysis of reading and learning to read* (3rd ed.). New York, NY: Holt, Rinehart, & Winston.

Snow, C. E., Burns, M. S., & Griffin, P. (Eds.). (1998). *Preventing reading difficulties in young children.* Washington, DC: National Academy Press.

Sperling, M. (1995). Uncovering the role of reading in writing and learning to write: One day in an inner-city classroom. *Written Communication, 12*(1), 93–133.

Stahl, S., & Miller, P. (1989). Whole language and language experience approaches for beginning reading: A quantitative research synthesis. *Review of Educational Research, 59,* 87–116.

Stanovich, K. E. (1986). Matthew effects in reading: Some consequences of individual differences in the acquisition of literacy. *Reading Research Quarterly, 21,* 360–406.

Stanovich, K. E. (2000). *Progress in understanding reading: Scientific foundations and new frontiers.* New York, NY: Guilford.

Stone, J., & Harris, K. (1991). These coloured spectacles: What are they for? *Support for Learning, 6,* 116–118.

Szatmari, P. (1992). The epidemiology of attention-deficit hyperactivity disorder. *Child and Adolescent Psychiatric Clinics of North America, 1,* 361–371.

Thomson, M. E., & Hartley, G. M. (1980). Self-concept in children with dyslexia. *Academic Therapy, 26,* 19–36.

Torgesen, J. K., Wagner, R. K., Rashotte, C. A., Rose, E., Lindamood, P., Conway, T., & Garvan, C. (1999). Preventing reading failure in young children with phonological processing disabilities: Group and individual responses to instruction. *Journal of Educational Psychology, 91,* 579–593.

Tur-Kaspa, H., Weisel, A., & Segev, L. (1998). Attributions for feelings of loneliness of students with learning disabilities. *Learning Disabilities Research and Practice, 13,* 89–94.

Vygotsky, L. S. (1978). *Mind in society.* Cambridge, MA: Harvard University Press.

Wenger, E. (1999). *Communities of practice: Learning, meaning and identity.* Cambridge, England: Cambridge University Press.

West, T. G. (1991). *In the mind's eye: Visual thinkers, gifted people with learning difficulties, computer images, and the ironies of creativity.* Buffalo, NY: Prometheus Books.

Wilcutt, E., & Pennington, B. (2000). Comorbidity of reading disability and attention-deficit/hyperactivity disorder: Differences by gender and subtype. *Journal of Learning Disabilities, 33,* 179–191.

Wilhelm, J. D. (1997). *"You gotta BE the book": Teaching engaged and reflective reading with adolescents.* New York, NY: Teachers College Press.

Worthy, J., & Prater, K. (2002). "I thought about it all night": Readers theatre for fluency and motivation. *The Reading Teacher, 56,* 294–297.

About the Author

Dr. Ellen Burns Hurst holds a Ph.D. in language and literacy and has spent a career focused on cutting-edge reading interventions in her clinical practice. A true pioneer in the field of dyslexia, Dr. Hurst continues to focus on her passion of changing the reading lives of students through her position as past-president of the International Dyslexia Association of Georgia, as an adjunct professor at Georgia State University, and through frequent research presentations at national and international literacy conferences.

Her research interests include a focus on the struggling reader in global school settings, as well as the social, cultural, and cognitive aspects of learning to read in the local classroom. As an experienced reading specialist in public schools, private school, and private practice, she has a theoretical and pragmatic interest in reading assessment and intervention. Her most current university teaching assignments at Georgia State University focus on assessment in the early childhood classroom for undergraduates, as well as literacy assessment and linguistic components of literacy at the graduate level.

Dr. Hurst is married to Michael Hurst, J.D., an attorney in private practice. They live in Atlanta, GA, where they share their passion for advocacy work for underachieving children.

Why Can't My Daughter Read?